IN SEARCH OF GUIDANCE

DEVELOPING A CONVERSATIONAL RELATIONSHIP WITH GOD

DALLAS WILLARD

Regal Books
A Division of GL Publications
Ventura, CA U.S.A.

Other Regal reading in the "In Search of . . ." series:
In Search of Dignity by R.C. Sproul
In Search of Certainty by John Guest

The translation of all Regal books is under the direction of GLINT. GLINT provides technical help for the adaptation, translation and publishing of books for millions of people worldwide. For information regarding translation contact: GLINT, P.O. Box 6688, Ventura, California 93006.

Published by Regal Books
A Division of GL Publications
Ventura, California 93006
Printed in U.S.A.

Library of Congress Cataloging in Publication data.

Willard, Dallas, 1935-
In search of guidance.

Includes bibliographical references.
1. Providence and government of God. 2.Fellowship
—Religious aspects—Christianity. I. Title.
BT135.W49 1983 231.7 83-17743
ISBN 0-8307-0899-5

TO JANE LAKES WILLARD

SWEET LADY,
GOOD SOLDIER,
FAITHFUL COMPANION ON THE WAY

CONTENTS

PREFACE

This book is written for those who believe that there is a personal God who is present in our world and cares about what we do. It does not attempt to *prove* that there is such a God, though it hopes to direct open-minded persons onto a path where they may find Him for themselves. Its thesis is that God has created man for fellowship with Himself, and that, as with fellowship between persons generally, He will *speak to* the individual human being when it is appropriate.

The model for divine guidance is therefore taken from what communication and guidance is at its best among human beings at *their* best. But "their best" is interpreted in the light of Jesus Christ and His followers. We should not judge the possibilities of humanity from a consideration of the dreary normalcy of human existence. Archbishop William Temple has wisely written:

> We do not know what Matter is when we look at

> Matter alone; only when Spirit dwells in Matter and uses it as a tool do we learn the capacities of Matter. The sensitiveness of eye and ear, the delicacy of the artist's touch, are achievements which we should never anticipate from the study of the lifeless. So, too, we do not know what Humanity really is, or of what achievements it is capable, until Divinity indwells in it. If we are to form a right conception of God we must look at Christ. The wise question is not, "Is Christ Divine?" but, "What is God like?" And the answer to that is "Christ." So, too, we must not form a conception of Humanity and either ask if Christ is Human or insist on reducing Him to the limits of our conception; we must ask, "What is Humanity?" and look at Christ to find the answer. We only know what Matter is when Spirit dwells in it; we only know what Man is when God dwells in him.[1]

Human guidance and communication in the light of Christ is, then, what provides us with our model or ideal picture of divine guidance. To take this seriously is to exclude all tricks, mechanical formulas, and gimmickry for "finding out what God wants me to do." Indeed, we hope to make it clear that the subject of divine guidance simply cannot be successfully treated in terms of *what God wants us to do* if that excludes—as it usually does—*what we want to do,* and even *what we want God to do.*

Being *in* the will of God, as paradoxical as this may seem, is very far removed from just doing what God wants us to do, as that is normally understood. So far removed, in fact, that we can be in the will of God, and know that we are, without knowing what God wants us to do. We can be in His will without His willing that we do any particular thing at all. Of course, we cannot fail to do what He specifically directs and still be in His will. And there are many ways of living and being that clearly are not in His will. Not just everything goes. But the serious inquirer after divine guidance must never forget that we could even do all He wants and commands, and still not be the person He would have us to be; for an obsession merely with *doing* all He commands may itself rule out our *being* the kind of person which He Himself is.

One of Jesus' parables is told to illuminate this point: "Will any one of you, who has a servant plowing or keeping sheep, say to him when he has come in from the field, 'Come at once and sit down at table'? Will he not rather say to him, 'Prepare supper for me, and gird yourself and serve me, till I eat and drink; and afterward you shall eat and drink'? Does he thank the servant because he did what was commanded? So you also, when you have done all that is commanded you, say, 'We are unworthy servants; we have only done what was our duty' " (Luke 17:7-10, *RSV*).

Much of what is said in this book is an elaboration of the point of this parable. I hope that it might be of *some* use for those who think only in terms of doing what they are commanded. But for all the good that is in that attitude it remains the attitude of the "unprofitable servant" when measured against the possibilities of fellowship with Jesus and His friends in the Kingdom of God.

The pages which follow deal with divine guidance as it bears upon a *life* in the will of God, upon the question of who God wants us *to be*—as well as, where appropriate, upon the question of what He wants us *to do.* What He wants us to do is, of course, very important; but it is never enough to allow us to understand our life before God, a life fully pleasing to Him.

Note

1. William Temple, "The Divinity of Christ," in *Foundations,* B.H. Streeter, ed. (London: Macmillan and Co., 1920), pp. 258-259.

CHAPTER 1

A "PARADOX" CONCERNING DIVINE GUIDANCE

There is not in the world a kind of life more sweet and delightful than that of a continual conversation with God. Those only can comprehend it who practice and experience it; yet I do not advise you to do it from that motive. It is not pleasure which we ought to seek in this exercise; but let us do it from a principle of love, and because God would have us (Brother Lawrence).

God Speaks to Me?

Sunday dinner was finished, but we lingered around the table savoring the good food and reflecting upon the morning's service at church. The congregation—where I then served as a very young and very green assistant pastor—was excited about its plans for a new sanctuary to replace its old building, much loved but long outgrown and overused.

The morning message had focused upon plans for a

new building. Our pastor spoke of his vision for the increased ministry of the church. He indicated how strongly he felt God's guidance in the way the congregation was going, and testified that God had spoken to him about things which should be done.

My wife's grandmother, Mrs. Lucy Latimer—"Mema" to us all—seemed deep in thought as we continued to chatter along. Finally she quietly said: "I wonder why God never speaks to me like that."

A simple comment, coming like a bolt out of the blue from the heart of this woman of unshakable faith and complete devotion, forever changed my attitude toward glib talk about God speaking to us or about divine guidance. In her words it was God who spoke to me. I had a vivid realization, which was never to leave me, of the extent to which such talk leaves many sincere Christians "on the outside looking in," or forces them to play at a game which they don't really understand and with which they feel extremely uncomfortable.

To that point in my own experience I had simply assumed that, if you were *really* Christian, God spoke to you as a matter of course. I was sure that He spoke individually and specifically about what He wanted each believer to do, and that He also taught and made real on an individual basis the general truths which all must believe in order to be saved and to live rightly before Him.

The Moving of God

Later I came to realize that this confidence came from a series of revival meetings in which I was immersed as a young man in high school. During those meetings I learned to interact with a characteristic type of thought and impulse which was to me the moving of God upon my mind and heart. It was an experience clearly marked out for me, though I had no theory about it. I later came to see that I really did not *understand* it at all. I only knew its reality, and thoughtlessly assumed that it was a functioning, intelligible fact in every believer's life.

Then as I subsequently grew into the Christian ministry, I learned to wait upon the word of God to come to me. In the most primary of senses, the word of God is simply *God speaking;* and I also learned to expect His speaking to come through me to others. Experience taught me the difference between when it was "just me" talking, or even "just me" quoting and discussing Scripture, and when a certain "something more" was taking place. Jeremiah's comparisons of God's Word to wheat over against the chaff, and to a fire, or to a hammer which crunches rock, all came to describe something with which I was very familiar (Jer. 23:28-29).

Such great Christians of the past as John Calvin[1] and William Law[2] had the ministry of Eli to me (1 Sam. 3:8-9) and helped me to understand what was happening to me. They helped me to identify and respond to the experience of *God speaking,* just as Eli helped Samuel, and they assured me that the same Spirit who delivered the Scriptures unto "holy men of old" speaks in the hearts of those who today gather around the Bible to minister and to be ministered unto. They also warned me that *only if* this happened could I avoid being just another clever "letter-learned scribe," trying to nourish the souls of my hearers on what *I* was able to understand by my own efforts from the Bible or elsewhere.

But it was not easy for me to understand that our most sacred experiences often blind us. The very light which makes it possible for us to see may also dazzle our eyes to the clearest of sights, or make it impossible to see what lies in a shadow. Caught up in the reality of the workings of God's voice I was for a long while unable to appreciate the huge problems which the very idea of God's speaking to us, of His guiding us in any way but the "providential," created for some of the most faithful adherents of the church—not to mention those entirely outside of it. When someone seemed to have difficulty with guidance, I passed it off as a sign of weakness of faith, or even of rebellion. I somehow could not face the fact that the very best of devout, faithful Christians often can make no sense of divine guidance which comes in a form other than the necessities imposed upon us by circumstances, thus turning all such guidance into blind force.

The Ongoing Conversation

Today I continue to believe that man is meant to live in an intermittent but ongoing conversation with God. The visits of God with Adam and Eve in the garden, Enoch's walks with God, the face-to-face conversations between Moses and Jehovah, are commonly regarded as highly exceptional moments in the religious history of mankind. Aside from their obvious historical significance, they are not meant to be that at all, in my opinion, but rather are examples of what normal human life was intended by God to be: the carnate habitation of a spiritual God, God indwelling His people through personal fellowship. Man lives—really lives—only by the constant speaking of God in his soul, or "by every word which proceeds out of the mouth of God."

During the months in which I have been engaged in the writing of this book, I have made a special point of drawing others out in conversation concerning their experiences with divine guidance. Many might be surprised to discover what a high percentage of serious Christians can tell of specific experiences in which God spoke to them. But the next thing one discovers is how rarely they speak about such experiences. Often they have never spoken of them at all, even to their closest friends. But when a spirit of acceptance is established, and it is clear that the topic is to be dealt with seriously, then the stories begin to flow. And as understanding and confidence grow, other cases come to mind which are seen to be or to contain a word from God to the individual.

But is it not with good reason that we often hesitate to

speak about these experiences which we yet feel compelled to describe as God speaking to us? Those who think they have sighted UFOs, or have had the after-death experiences much discussed in recent years, soon learn to keep their mouths shut. They know that they may single themselves out for unwanted attention if they are not very careful. Perhaps they will be regarded as crazy. And since such experiences really are strange and very hard to interpret, they genuinely fear being misguided. They do not wish to "go public" with something that might just be a mistake on their part. They also fear being thought of as arrogant, as taking themselves to be someone special or, to borrow language from the Apostle Paul, as being "exalted above measure through the abundance of the revelations" (2 Cor. 12:7).

Similar doubts and hesitations may well trouble those who are spoken to by God. This is especially true since there generally is little specific teaching or pastoral guidance available in such matters. Indeed, some churches discourage the thought that God *would* speak to the individual; and some leaders may prefer that He speak only to them and not to their flock. After all it is well known that people go off into all sorts of errors and become quite unmanageable once God starts talking to them.

For Leaders Only?

Faced with such inner fears and such a lack of teaching—or even with explicit denial or discouragement—the disciple of Christ today is then further confused by another message which comes from his surroundings. For one also is constantly confronted with suggestions or implications that *ideally* we *should* be engaged in communications with God, just like our leaders. Certainly, they do commonly say that God speaks to them; and *because they're* our leaders, we should strive to be like them. Here are a few cases selected almost at random:

The internationally known Methodist evangelist and

faith healer Oral Roberts recently informed his audiences that he had had a seven-hour talk with Jesus through which, "in that calm voice I have heard so many times before," he received instructions for a fund-raising plan that would lead to a discovery of a cure for cancer.[3]

David Wilkerson, highly successful and well-known author and minister, records that in the summer of 1973 he had "a vision of five tragic calamities coming upon the earth. I saw no blinding lights, I heard no audible voices, nor did I hear from an angel. While I was in prayer late one night, these visions of world calamities came over me with such impact that I could do nothing but kneel, transfixed, and take it all in."[4]

On a television interview of January 31, 1983, Dr. Ken Taylor, who produced the widely used version of the Bible known as *The Living Bible,* told how he had been concerned about children having a Bible which they could easily understand. According to his statement, one afternoon "God revealed" to him "the idea of a thought-for-thought translation instead of word-for-word." This idea worked so well that such versions have now been published in many languages around the world.

Joyce Landorf, one of the most popular current Christian writers and speakers, tells in a recent book about her struggle with one of her daughters who was engaged in an unhappy love relationship. For four years the struggle continued. Then, "in November of that fourth year, I told the Lord that Thanksgiving would be the day we would all talk to Laurie. We, as her immediate family, would tell her she had to break off this devastating relationship. We would not stand by and watch her go over a cliff and destroy herself any longer. I asked the Lord for the right words. Instead of giving me the appropriate remarks, He commanded sternly, 'Be quiet.'

"I told Him I didn't think He knew how long this had gone on or how serious the whole thing had become, and asked again what He wanted me to say. Once more, the

Lord said, 'I want you to be quiet.' "

But she wasn't quiet. She disobeyed her instructions and it led to a severe alienation between her daughter Laurie and the rest of the family. Laurie walked out. Mrs. Landorf records that then "Clearly I heard the Lord say, 'I *told* you to be quiet.' "[5]

Commonly, in times of great inward distress, we hear the voice of God directed specifically to us. In the 1640s George Fox, founder of the Friends or Quaker movement, wandered the fields and byways of the English countryside, seeking someone who could show him the way to peace with God. But he finally became convinced that "there was none among them all that could speak to my condition. And when all my hopes in them and in all men were gone, so that I had nothing outwardly to help me, nor could I tell what to do; then, oh! then I heard a voice which said, 'there is one, even Christ Jesus, that can speak to thy condition'; and when I heard it, my heart did leap for joy. Then the Lord did let me see why there was none upon the earth that could speak to my condition, namely, that I might give Him all the glory."[6]

A weekly publication from a large local church tells us that the pastor "has been given a bold vision by our Lord." The vision is that every person in the entire geographical area where the church is located should be called to Christ in a one-year period by a telephone call from some person in the church. This is not described as a bright idea which struck the pastor, but as a vision communicated to him by God. And of course that makes all the difference in the world in its meaning for the congregation which the pastor leads.

Now I cite these cases here, not because they are exceptional, but precisely because they are so common. There is a practically endless supply of such cases. They vary in detail as we move from one denominational tradition to another, but they are in some degree present in all Christian communions except those that are so theologically liberal as to verge into simple humanism. (I should add that, to my surprise, I have often found even in those groups many people to whom "talking with God" is an ordinary event.)

But then we should expect nothing else, given the words of the scriptural record and the heritage of the Christian Church. As Christians we stand in a millenia-long tradition of man being addressed by God. The ancient Israelites heard the voice of their God speaking to them out of the midst of fire (Deut. 4:33). A regular place of communion and conversational interchange between the high priest and God was established in the "mercy seat" over the ark of God (Exod. 25:22; see also Luke 1:11-21).

But the individual man of faith among the Israelites also cried out expectantly to be taught by God: "Teach me to do thy will; for thou art my God: thy spirit is good; lead me into the land of uprightness" (Ps. 143:10). The experience of Israel led the prophet Isaiah—who had firsthand experience in conversing with God (Isa. 6)—to describe conditions of the faithful in which "then shalt thou call, and the Lord shall answer; thou shalt cry, and he shall say, Here I am . . . . And the Lord shall guide thee continually" (Isa. 58:9,11).

"Abiding" Includes Conversing

On the evening before His crucifixion, Jesus assured His little band of followers that although He was leaving them He would continue to "manifest" Himself to all who loved Him. The Judas who was also called Thaddeus (not Iscariot) then asked just the right question: *How* would this "manifesting" take place? Jesus' reply was that He and His Father "will come unto him, and make our abode with him" (John 14:23).

Now it may well be that the abiding of the Son and the Father in the faithful heart involves more than conscious communication or conversation; but it surely *does* involve that, in the manner and measure our Lord deems appropriate. It is simply beyond belief that two *persons* so intimately related as indicated by Jesus in His answer to Thaddeus would not *speak* with each other. The Spirit which inhabits us is not dumb, restricting Himself to an occasional nudge, a hot flash, or a case of goose bumps.

Such simple reasonings add a further weight to the examples set by well-known Christians, confirming us in the thought that ideally we should be engaged in personal communion with God. And we might well ask: How *could* there be *personal* relationships, a personal walk, with God—or with any other person—without individualized communication?

Sometimes today it seems that our personal relationship with God is spoken of us as a mere "arrangement" or "understanding" between Jesus and His Father *about* us. Our "personal relationship" then only means that each believer has his or her own unique "account" in heaven which allows them to draw upon the merits of Christ to pay their sin bills. Or possibly it means that God's general providence for His creation is adequate to provide for each person. But who does not think that there should be much more to a *personal* relationship than that? A mere benefactor, however powerful, kind, and thoughtful, is not the same thing as a *friend.* "But I have called you friends" (John 15:15).

One-to-One with God

In the last analysis nothing is more central to the practical life of the Christian than confidence in God's individual dealings with each person on a one-to-one basis. The individual care of the shepherd for his sheep, of the father for his child, and of the lover for the beloved are all biblical images that have passed into the fundamental consciousness of Western humanity in its art and general culture as well as through its religion. Not only conservative and liberal Christians, high-church and pentecostal, but also Christian and Jew, and even Jew and Muslim, come together in saying: "The Lord is *my* shepherd; *I* shall not want. *He* maketh *me* to lie down in green pastures: *he* leadeth *me* beside the still waters" (Ps. 23:1-2, italics added).

The biblical record always presents relationships between God and the believer as more like friendships or familial ties than mere arrangements by one person for the needs of another. If we pass before our minds that startling array of biblical personalities from Adam to Paul the apostle, we behold the millenia-long saga of God Himself invading human personality and history on a one-to-one basis. There is nothing "general" or secondhand about the divine encounters with Abraham, Moses, Isaiah, Nehemiah, Mary, or Peter.

The saga continues up to our own day in the lives of those recognized as leaders in the spiritual life. When, coming through the ages, we consider a Saint Augustine, a Saint Francis of Assisi, a Martin Luther, a George Fox, a John Wesley, a C.H. Spurgeon, a D.L. Moody, a Frank Laubach, or an A.W. Tozer, we see in each case persons for whom personal communion *and* communication with God are regarded both as life-changing episodes *and* as daily bread.

Untold thousands of humble Christians whose names will never appear in print, who will never preach a sermon, never lead a crusade, could equally well testify to exactly the same kinds of encounters with God as are manifested in the great ones in The Way.

Robert C. McFarlane moved to California in 1970, and within just a few days from his arrival—due to a most unfortunate misunderstanding with a very close, lifelong friend—fell heir to an insurance agency which he did not want but which he *had* to make succeed in order to save his investment. By the spring of 1973 he was in the third straight year of constant strain and stress in the operation of the business. He had recently been converted under the ministry of the Rolling Hills Covenant Church in Southern California, in answer to the prayers of his wife, Betty, and her many Christian friends. But one day that spring the continual facing of defeat, the daylight and dark hours of effort, frustration at every turn, and the hardened memories of the cause of his financial difficulties weighed heavily upon him. Robert drove toward his office, facing *another* day of futility and failure, but having to accomplish the absolute necessities to keep the business afloat. Suddenly he was filled with a frantic urge to turn left onto the Harbor Freeway—and just disappear. To this day he honestly feels he was going to *make* the turn. How far he would have gone is of course unknown. But, be that as it may, into the midst of his inner turmoil there came a command: "PULL OVER TO THE CURB." As he relates it, it was as if the words were written on the windshield. After pulling over there came to him, as from someone in the car with him, these words: "My Son had strains that you will never know, and when He had those strains He turned to me, and that's what *you* should do." After hearing these words Robert sat at the wheel for a long time, sobbing aloud. He then drove on to his Long Beach office where, during that day—whether it concerned company disagreements, agency clients deciding to remain with his agency, payments by clients of sizeable, late premiums, or whatever—of the remembered number of twenty-two major problems, *all* pertinent ones were substantially resolved by that day's end.

In the more scholarly vein, Wilhelm Hermann, a theologian of the late nineteenth century, goes so far as to mark the Christian out in terms of a personal communion with God. "We hold a man to be really a Christian when we believe we have ample evidence that God has revealed Himself to him in Jesus Christ, and that now the man's inner life is taking on a new character through his communion with the God who is thus manifest."[7]

More recently the English philosopher and theologian John Baillie writes: "Our knowledge of God rests on the revelation of His personal presence . . . . Of such a presence it must be true that to those who have never been confronted with it argument is useless, while to those who have, it is superfluous."[8]

The faith in a God who speaks personally to the soul is nowhere recorded more plainly than in the hymns of the Church, from all ages, sung week by week as the Church congregates, and day by day as Christians go about their individualized ways at work, at home, at play: "Saviour, Like a Shepherd Lead Us," "All the Way My Saviour Leads Me," "Lead On, O King Eternal," "Where He Leads Me," "Lead Kindly Light," "He Leadeth Me," "Holy Spirit, Faithful Guide," "Jesus Saviour, Pilot Me," "If Thou But Suffer God to Guide Thee," "Guide Me, O Thou Great Jehovah," "Jesus, Still Lead On."

This brief list hardly begins to mention all of the hymns devoted to personal divine guidance and the conversational communion of the soul with God.

> He walks with me, and he talks with me,
> And he tells me I am His own,
> And the joy we share as we tarry there,
> None other has ever known.[9]

The Paradox

In the light of all this it is not an exaggeration to speak of a *paradox* in the contemporary experience of divine guidance.

On the one hand, there is massive testimony to and widespread faith in God's personal, not merely providential, guidance, often thought of as accomplished by conscious communication *from* God *to* us. This is not only recorded in Scripture and emblazoned upon the history of the Church. It also lies at the heart of our worship services, of our personal relationship with God, and serves as the basis of authority in our teachers and leaders. Only rarely will one find a minister who professes to teach and lead the flock of God on the basis of his education, natural talents, and denominational connections alone. Authority in spiritual leadership derives only from life in the Spirit, from the minister's personal encounter and ongoing relationship with God.

But on the other hand, we also find a pervasive and often painful uncertainty concerning how divine guidance works and what its place is in the Church and in the Christian's life. Even those who firmly believe that they have been addressed or directly spoken to by God may be at a loss to know what is happening or what to do about it.

Poor flustered Gideon said to the Lord who in some fashion stood before him: "Do something to prove that you are the one who is speaking to me!" (see Judg. 6:17). Even if we have begged for a word from God we may have so little clarity on what it should be like when it comes, and so little competence in dealing with it, that it will only add to our confusion. I believe that this is one reason why such a word may be withheld from us when it otherwise would be appropriate.

The need for understanding is clearly very great. We are all too familiar with the painful confusion of individuals—once again, they are frequently the most sincere and devout—in their efforts to determine God's will for them. We see them make dreadful errors following a whim or chance event which, because of their desperation, they *will* to be a sign from God. We see them sink into despair, skepticism, even cynicism; often accompanied by a continuation of religious routine, but now utterly mechanical and dead. They "know" on the basis of what has happened to them that for all practical purposes they are *simply on their own.*

And we are also all too familiar, if we only read the newspapers, with the tragic domination of groups by those who lay claim to a special sign or word from God. They cannot be effectively withstood because the other members of the group have no clear idea, tested and proven in experience, of how such a word really works. They are vulnerable to madness in the name of God.

Toward a Solution

Now I believe we cannot, as disciples of Jesus Christ, abandon our faith in God's personal guidance of our minds and lives. The "paradox" of divine guidance must then be resolved and removed by providing the believer with a clear understanding and a confident practical orientation toward God's way of guiding us and communicating with us. In order to provide this, however, three general problem areas must be dealt with.

First, what we know about guidance and the divine-human encounter from the Bible, church history, and the lives of the great ones in The Way shows that *God's communications come to us in many forms.* This is appropriate to the complexity of human personality and cultural history as well as to the fact that God in redemption must reach out to man who is in a fallen and weakened condition. But we must carefully look at these many forms to see which ones are most suited to the *kind* of relationship which God intends to have with His people. If we give primacy to forms of communication which God does not on the whole prefer in relation to His children, that will hinder our understanding of and cooperation with His guidance—perhaps even totally frustrating it. One of the main tasks of the chapters which follow is to prevent this.

Second, *there is a problem in the area of motivation.* We all in some measure share the general human anxiety about the future. We by nature live in the future, constantly hurled into it whether we like it or not. Knowing what we will meet there is a condition of our being prepared to deal with it. Or so it would seem from the human point of view. Francis Bacon's saying that knowledge is power is never more vividly realized than in our concern about our own future. So we ceaselessly inquire about the future. The great businesses and the halls of government are filled with experts and technocrats, our modern-day magicians and soothsayers; and a new discipline of "futureology" has recently emerged within the universities. The age-old trades of palm reading and fortune-telling flourish.[10]

Within the Christian community, teaching on the will of God and how to know it continues to be one of the most popular subjects. Russ Johnston draws upon his own wide experience to remark:

> A certain church I know has elective Sunday School classes for their adults. Every three months they choose a new topic to study. The pastor tells me that if they can have someone teach on knowing God's will, they can run that class over and over, and still people sign up for it in droves.
>
> I've spoken at many conferences where part of the afternoons are set aside for workshops on various topics. If you make one of the workshops "Knowing the Will of God," half the people sign up for it even if there are 20 other choices.[11]

But is there not at work here a self-defeating motive which causes people to take these classes and workshops over and over without coming to peace about their place in the will of God? My own observations suggest that many persons seek the will of God as a manipulative device for securing their own safety, comfort, and righteousness. Even for those who busy themselves to know the will of God, however, it is still true that "whosoever will save his life shall lose it" (Matt. 16:25). Extreme preoccupation with knowing the will of God "for me" may only indicate, contrary to what is often thought, an over concern with myself, not a Christlike interest in the well-being of others or the glory of God. F.B. Meyer writes: "So long as there is some thought of personal advantage, some idea of acquiring the praise and commendation of men, some aim of self-aggrandisement, it will be simply impossible to find out God's purpose concerning us."[12] Nothing will go right in the search for guidance if this false motivation is its foundation. In the chapters to follow we must make clear a different type of motivation for knowing God's guidance and listening to His voice.

Third, a truly overwhelming problem blocks understanding of divine guidance when *we misconceive the very nature of our heavenly Father and of His intent for us* as His redeemed children and friends. From this then comes a further misunderstanding of what the Church, His redemptive community, is to be like, and especially of how *authority* works in the Kingdom of God.

God certainly is not a jolly good fellow, nor is He our "buddy." But then neither are we intended by Him to be robots wired into His instrument panel, puppets on His string, or slaves dancing at the end of the whiplash of His command. Such ideas must not serve as the basis for our view of divine guidance.

A Conversational Relationship

The ideal for divine guidance is finally determined by who God is, and who we are, and what a personal relationship between ourselves and God should be like. Failure of competence in dealing with divine guidance has its *deepest* root in a failure to understand, accept and grow into a conversational relationship with God: that sort of relationship suited to friends who are mature personalities in a shared enterprise, no matter how different they may be in other respects.

It is within such a relationship that our Lord surely intends us to have, and readily to recognize, His voice speaking in our hearts as occasion demands. I believe that He has made ample provision for this in order to fulfill His mission as the Good Shepherd, which is to bring us life and life more abundantly. The abundance of life comes in following Him, and "the sheep follow him: for they know his voice" (John 10:4).

We now begin to deal with these problem areas which confront our search for divine guidance by looking at some general but essential preliminary guidelines to guidance.

Questions

1. Does God "speak" to you? Are you sure?

2. *Can* God speak to all Christians? all people? in what way(s)?

3. What is the "paradox" about divine guidance which is discussed in this chapter? What three problems must be dealt with? How?

4. What are some reasons that people might resist a "conversational relationship" with God? Are any of them good reasons? If you reject such a relationship, what are your reasons?

5. Does "abiding" need to include "conversing"? Why?

6. Why do many have no difficulty with letting their leaders be "spoken to" by God, while they themselves shun such a possibility?

7. Do you have a "conversational relationship" with God? If not, do you *want* one?

Notes

1. *Institutes of the Christian Religion,* Henry Beveridge, Translator (Grand Rapids: Wm. B. Eerdmans Publishing Co., 1975). Book I, Chapter VII.

2. *The Power of the Spirit* (Fort Washington, PA: Christian Literature Crusade, 1971), Chapter V.

3. News section of *Christianity Today,* February 18, 1983, p. 29.

4. David Wilkerson, *The Vision* (Old Tappan, NJ: Fleming H. Revell Co., 1974), p. 11.

5. Joyce Landorf, *Change Points* (Old Tappan, NJ: Fleming H. Revell Co., 1981), pp. 156-157.

6. George Fox, *The Journal of George Fox* (London: J.M. Dent & Sons, Ltd., 1948), pp. 8-9.

7. Wilhelm Hermann, *The Communion of the Christian with God,* 3rd English ed. (London: Williams and Norgate, 1909), p. 14.

8. John Baillie, *Our Knowledge of God* (New York: Charles Scribners Sons, 1959), p. 132.

9. "In the Garden," by C. Austin Miles, chorus.

10. J.A. Sargent, "Astrology's Rising Star," *Christianity Today,* February 4, 1983, pp. 37-39.

11. Russ Johnston, *How to Know the Will of God* (Colorado Springs: Navpress, 1971), p. 5.

12. Frederick B. Meyer, *The Secret of Guidance* (Chicago: Moody Press, n.d.), p. 12.

CHAPTER 2

GUIDELINES TO GUIDANCE

He brought me to the banqueting house, and his banner over me was love . . . . Eat, O friends, and drink: drink deeply, O lovers! (Song of Solomon, 2:4;5:1, RSV*)*

The Perfectly Guided Wife

You may have seen *The Stepford Wives*. It is the story of a couple, probably in their early or middle thirties, who move into an upper middle-class community called Stepford, where the men are mostly workers in high technology businesses and industries.

The wife soon notices that the greater percentage of the other Stepford wives uniformly exhibit very strange behavior patterns. They are continuously ecstatic over sewing, cleaning their houses, manicuring their lawns, and baking cookies. When they get together they mainly trade recipes, or coo over their clean floors and latest triumphs in making their husbands' lives more comfortable. They never fight or are unpleasant with anyone, but especially not with their husbands—and they have no opinions or interests which reach beyond their family, home, and club.

There are a few of the wives who remain on the feisty, individualistic side; but they have a tendency to leave for a "vacation" with their husband and, upon returning, to dwell upon cookies and clean floors just like the rest. When this happens to the best friend of our most recent Stepford wife—who was already very suspicious abut what was going on—she becomes desperate and stabs her old friend with a knife to see if she will bleed. She doesn't! She merely repeats pathetic little maneuvers around her kitchen, mouthing the same inane niceties over and over, while her frightened friend backs away and runs out the door.

By this time, however, her own robot replacement is almost ready. In the end we see her (or it) with the placid robot look on her face, ready to wear frilly blouses and aprons, make cookies, grow ecstatic over clean floors, and be sweet, *sweet,* SWEET: the perfectly guided wife!

The message of *The Stepford Wives* is obvious, but one which is frequently forgotten: In close personal relationships conformity to another's wishes, be it ever so perfect, is *not* desirable, if it is mindless, purchased at the expense of freedom, and destructive of personality. This is not a truth which can be set aside when we come to think about God's relationships to His human creation.

The Context of Guidance

Specifically, this means that in our attempts to understand how God guides us we must above all hold to the fact that guidance is to be sought *only as a part of a certain kind of life:* a life of loving fellowship with the King and His subjects within the Kingdom of God. We must never forget that God's guidance for us, whatever it may be in its initial stages of our experience, is intended to develop into an intelligent, freely cooperative relationship between mature persons who love each other. We must therefore make our primary goal not just to have the guidance of God, but to be such persons in such a relationship to Him. Only so will guidance itself come right. This is our *first* general guideline to guidance.

Love: A Way of "Being With"

When we love someone, we of course want to do what they wish. But this is not just in order to avoid trouble or gain favor. It is a way of *being with* them, of sharing their life and their person. The gushing pleasure of the small child who is "helping mama" comes from the expansion of his little self through immersion in the life of a larger self to which he is lovingly abandoned. *With* mother he does "big things" which he could not undertake on his own; but he would not even be interested in doing them apart from her or her interest, attention, and affection.

The sense of larger power and larger life that comes to adults when they enjoy requited love is also a valid perception of that expansion of self through identification with another which comes when, in the manner appropriate to the persons involved, two become one.

When the two are one, the beloved who also loves does not want to be in the position of forever ordering the lover-beloved about: "Do this for me! Do that for me!" The less of that the better, and he or she would like to be understood in a manner which would make it completely unnecessary. To be always telling the other what to do is simply not compatible with that union of souls—that sweet repose upon, that conscious delight and rest in another—which is the highest act and most exalted condition possible between persons.

And this is true with God also who is a person loving and beloved. Our highest calling and opportunity in life is to love Him with all our being. And He has loved us so much that His only Son was given up to death in order to save us. In the light of this great redemptive fact we immeasurably demean Him by casting Him in the role of the cosmic boss, foreman, autocrat, whose chief joy in relation to men is ordering them around and taking pleasure in their conformity to His commands, painstakingly noting any departures.

Now I have no doubt at all that a record *is* kept, written automatically in the texture of our souls and the surrounding universe, and readable when occasion demands. But the ideal of God for His family is clearly something very different from the relation of a boss to his subordinates, and was expressed by Jesus in His prayer: "That they may all be one; even as thou, Father, art in me, and I in thee, that they also may be in us" (John 17:21, *RSV*). We are to be friends (2 Chron. 20:7; John 15:13-15) and fellow workers (1 Cor. 3:9) with God.

God As Taskmaster

Far too commonly, no doubt, we think of God as did the man in the Parable of the Talents, who regarded his lord as "a hard man," was accordingly afraid of him, and proudly, in his blindness, gave him back exactly what "belonged" to him (Matt. 25:14-30). Such a one *cannot* "enter into the joy of his lord" because—misconceiving of their relationship as he did—he could not enter into his lord's mind and life nor open his own life to his lord. He actually *abused* his lord by taking him to be interested only in getting "what was coming to him," while the lord for his part was really interested in sharing his life and goods with others.

The role of taskmaster, pleased *or* angry, is one that God accepts only on man's mean and ungenerous appointment. He thus often condescends to us because *our* consciousness (so clouded as it is by our experiences in a fallen world with "superiors," whether they be parents, bosses, kings, or those who stand over us in manipulative "love") cannot rise any higher. And the rule then is, as always: "As is your faith, so be it unto you." (See Matt.

8:13.) Better *some* relation to God than no relation at all!

But when we come in search of divine guidance, we must be sure to come in such a way that we do justice to the revelation of God in Christ. Guidance is an almost universal human preoccupation, and it is hard to cleanse our minds of those motives, images, and conceptualizations which would brutalize the very God whom we hope to approach. From primitive ritual to the "Bible roulette" so common among present-day believers, we see both the desperate urgency and superstitious character of human efforts to get a word from God on what is going to happen and what we should do. If necessary, to *force* it from Him or someone else. We *will have* our own peculiar "witch of Endor" (1 Sam. 28).

Here as elsewhere we must take with utmost seriousness Jesus' words: "No one knows the Father except the Son and those to whom the Son chooses to reveal him" (Matt. 11:27, *JB*). And this means, above all else, that the conscious seeking of divine guidance is safe and sensible only within that life of experiential union with God in His Kingdom which Jesus Christ brought to light in His own person and passed on in His continuing incarnation, the Church.

Divine guidance cannot be ours as a reliable and intelligible fact of life except when seen as one aspect of God's presence with us and of His life in us. Only our *communion* with God provides the appropriate context of *communications* between us and Him. And within those communications *guidance* is given in a manner suitable to our particular lives and circumstances and to our life together with Him in His earthly and heavenly family. To repeat, this is our first preliminary insight to guide us in our search for divine guidance.

Merely Human?

"And when the people saw what Paul had done, they shouted out . . . 'The gods are come down to us in the likeness of men,' . . . and would have done sacrifice . . . . But Barnabas and Paul ran in among the people, saying, 'Sirs, why do ye these things? We also are men of like passions with you'" (see Acts 14:11-15).

A second truth which is preliminary to any successful attempt to understand divine guidance concerns the relationship of *our* experience to the contents of the Bible—and, by extension, to the lives of the saints and heroes of the faith throughout the ages. The scene just given through a quotation from the book of Acts portrays the common human response to anyone who is living in that close relationship with God which marks them out by special manifestations of the divine presence in their lives. We immediately think: *They just aren't human!* By which we mean that their experience—including their experience of God—is not like ours, and perhaps that they are even a special *kind* of person, so that our experience of God never *could* be like theirs.

It is hard to believe that someone caught up in the life of God could still be human. One of the most serious and severe doctrinal struggles in the early Church was over whether Jesus was authentically human. A primary function of the doctrine of the virgin birth, when first introduced, was to secure the fact that Jesus really did have a human body, since He was literally *born* of a woman. His body came forth from a womb.[1] Still earlier, in the days of His flesh, when His humanity was quite visible through His literal bodily presence and processes, His closest friends and associates apparently could not see His divinity. Philip, as the end drew near, said, "Lord, show us the Father and that will be enough." Jesus could only reply, "Have I been so long time with you, and yet hast thou not known me, Philip? he that hath seen me hath seen the Father" (John 14:8-9).

He was *human,* yet divine; *divine,* yet human. It is fairly easy to say, but only the gracious assistance of God enables us to base our lives upon it.

This problem of uniting the life of God with the life of humanity continued to bother the early believers. Elijah was cited by James (5:17) as a case well known which could help them understand their own experience and its possibilities. The story of his terror before Jezebel, of his running for his life, of his dissolving into a mass of righteous self-pity (1 Kings 19), shows clearly that he *really was* human, "a man subject to like passions as we are" (Jas. 5:17), regardless of his fantastic feats in the power of God. We can tell his story from the inside, if we have any imagination at all, because we know how it would have been for us.

Just imagine *yourself* rising before a joint session of Congress, or standing before the President and nationwide television in the White House Rose Garden. Imagine saying there that it would not rain until *you* said so. Think of disappearing amid incredulous snickers, probably escorted by the police, and then of being dismissed as a harmless crackpot. Think of becoming one of the FBI's ten "most wanted," or your picture going up on "wanted" posters, of being regarded as endangering national security. Then you reappear. Now before a *worldwide* television audience you call down fire from heaven, gun down the false leaders of the country, and ride down Madison Avenue to a ticker-tape parade!

While enjoying a rally in your honor in Yankee Stadium or the Rose Bowl, word comes that the most powerful men in your country will kill you within twenty-four hours. How do you feel then? Then what do you do? Probably just what Elijah did.

The Problem of Success

Later events show that Elijah became obsessed with *himself*. "*I*, even *I only*, am left" (1 Kings 19:14, italics added). *His* success had cut him off from God—God who *was* his success. So when Jezebel said, "I'm going to get *you*," his mind no longer reached out to God, for it was absorbed wholly in himself. He really was like the rest of us. For us human beings it is not suffering, it is not failure which is the graduate course in the spiritual life. It is success. The passions to which Elijah was subjected in his success closed the eye of his faith so that he could no longer see the God with whom he had worked to withhold rain and bring down fire from heaven.

The humanity of Elijah, of Paul, of Peter, of Jesus Christ Himself, of all that wonderful company of riotously human women and men whose experience is recorded in the Bible and in the history of the Church, is to teach us one important lesson: Our humanity will not by itself prevent us from knowing and interacting with God as they did.

Conversely, if we are really to understand the Bible record itself, we must enter into our study of it on the assumption that the experiences recorded were basically the same as ours would be if we were there. Otherwise, the things which happened to the people in the Bible will be unreal to us. We will not be able to believe the Bible because it will have no experiential substance for us. It will mean nothing concrete, and our blindness will shut the door upon those tender overtures of God which invite our souls to communion with Him (Rev. 3:20). We will be left without the God-provided scriptural keys to interpreting our own encounters with Him, and will, like Balaam, be unable to recognize the angels standing directly in our path (Num. 22).

Failure to read the Bible in this way accounts for two common problems in Christian groups which hold the Bible central to their faith. One is that it becomes simply a book of doctrine, of abstract truth *about* God, which one can endlessly search without encountering God Himself or hearing His voice. This same attitude led the religious authorities of Jesus' own day to use the Scriptures for the very purpose of *avoiding Him.* They fervently searched the Scriptures, yet Jesus said of them: "Ye have not his word abiding in you" (John 5:38).

A. W. Tozer has pointedly remarked, in this connection:

> It is altogether possible to be instructed in the rudiments of the faith and still have no real understanding of the whole thing. And it is possible to go on to become expert in Bible doctrine and not have spiritual illumination, with the result that a veil remains over the mind, preventing it from apprehending the truth in its spiritual essence."[2]

The other problem which arises when we do not understand the experience of biblical characters in terms of our own is that we simply stop reading the Bible altogether. Or else we take it "in regular doses," choking it down like medicine, because someone tells us that it will be good for us—though we really do not find it to be so.

The open secret of many "Bible believing" churches is that only a very small percentage of their members study the Bible with even that degree of interest or intelligence which they bring to bear upon their newspaper or *Time* magazine. In my opinion, based upon considerable experience, this is primarily because they do not and are not taught how to understand the experience of biblical characters in terms of their own experience. Perhaps they are even warned not to so understand it. But that we are to understand the Bible in terms of our own experience is exactly what the Bible itself is teaching when it says that Paul, Barnabas, and Elijah were "subject to like passions as we are," and that Jesus is touched with the feeling of our infirmities because He Himself "was in all points tempted like as we are" (Heb. 4:15).

If we are to understand divine guidance for ourselves and on an individual basis we must, above all else, observe *how* the word of God came to those persons described in the Scriptures. How was it that they experienced God's communication? We must prayerfully but boldly use our God-given imaginations to fill out the reality of the events concerned in terms of what it would be like if *we* were Moses standing by the bush (Exod. 3:2), little Samuel lying in his darkened room (1 Sam. 3:3-7), Elisha under inspiration from the minstrel (2 Kings 3:15), Ananias receiving his vision about Paul (Acts 9:11), or Peter on his rooftop (Acts 10:10). We must pray for the faith and for the experiences which would enable us to believe that *such* things *could* happen to us. Only so will we be able to accept them and dwell in them when they come. This is our second general guideline to guidance.

Humble Arrogance: Who, Me, Lord?

"Notwithstanding in this rejoice not, that the spirits are subject unto you; but rather rejoice, because your names are written in heaven" (Luke 10:20).

The script of Richard Attenborough's *Gandhi* has a section where the young Indian lawyer and a white clergyman are walking together on the boardwalk, contrary to South African law at the time. They are accosted by some brutish looking young white men who seem about to harm them. But the mother of the ringleader calls from an upstairs window and commands him to go about his business. As they walk on, the clergyman exclaims over their good *luck,* but Gandhi comments: "I thought you were a man of God." The clergyman replies: "I am, but I don't believe He plans His day around me!"

The audience laughs. A cute point. But beneath it lies an attitude and a set of beliefs which may make it impossible for us to take seriously the possibility of divine guidance. And if we do not take it seriously, then of course we shall not be able to enter into it.

To the statement made above, that we must think of ourselves as capable of having the same kinds of experiences as Elijah or Paul, many will spontaneously reply: "But who am I to put myself in the place of these great ones? Who am I even to suppose that God might guide *me* or speak to me, much less that my experience should be like that of a Moses or Elisha?" Such a reaction poses as one which does honor to the greatness of God, but in fact it contradicts what God has taught about Himself in the Bible and in the person of Christ. His greatness is precisely what allows Him to plan His day around me and everyone else, as He chooses.

Within the scriptural record, those spoken to by God such as Moses or Gideon often tried to plead unworthiness or inadequacy. While such responses are in a sense fitting, they are also beside the point. We might even find it hard to believe if we were told that the president of the United States or some other merely human dignitary had called to talk to us. We think on the one hand that we are not *that* important; and on the other hand, that such a communication might seem to *make* us important. Similar thoughts may be stirred up at the suggestion of God talking to us. But they are simply irrelevant to His purposes in dealing with us; and moreover they are tragically false notions with the power to shut us off from the individualized guidance of God.

In the first place, *we are that important.* We were important enough for God to give His Son's life for us and choose to inhabit us as a living temple. Obviously, then, we are important enough for Him to guide us and speak to us where that is appropriate.

And in the second place, *His speaking to us does not in itself make us important.* It also does not make us righteous or infallible. Like the ancient people of Israel, it simply gives us greater opportunity and responsibility. Divine/human conversation is merely one aspect of that multifaceted personal interaction for which man was created in the first place, through which the sweet society of God's own trinitarian personality is extended towards the maximum goodness and glory possible in the created universe.

But there is another side to all of this. While being spoken to by God does not by itself make *us* anything special, if we allow it (or anything else, for that matter) to make us *think* we are something great, guidance will quite certainly be withdrawn. Moses may well be the all-time record holder for lengthy conversations with God. If there were such a category in the *Guinness Book of World Records,* he would certainly head the list. But he was also one of the least presumptuous men who ever walked the earth: "Now the man Moses was very meek, more than all men that were on the face of the earth" (Num. 12:3, *RSV*). There certainly was a connection between his meekness and his close working and talking relationship with God. Psalm 25:9 states: "The meek will he guide in judgment: and the meek will he teach his way."

The Strength of True Meekness

In his book *George Müeller of Bristol,* A. T. Pierson comments on this verse in a way which both elaborates the present point and will prove useful for our later discussions:

> Here is a double emphasis upon *meekness* as a condition of such guidance and teaching. *Meekness is a real preference for God's will.* Where this holy habit of mind exists, the whole being becomes so open to impression that, without any *outward* sign or token, there is an *inward* recognition and choice of the will of God. God guides, not by a visible sign, but by *swaying the judgment.* To wait before Him, weighing candidly in the scales every consideration for or against a proposed course, and in readiness to see which way the preponderance lies, is a frame of mind and heart in which one is fitted to be guided; and God touches the scales and makes the balance to sway as He will. *But our*

> *hands must be off the scales,* otherwise we need expect no interposition of His, in our favour.[3]

So the third preliminary truth which we must keep constantly before us in search of divine guidance is: *God does not speak to us because we are particularly great or good, nor does His speaking to us make us so.* We should extend this point onward to say that when God speaks to us that does not prove that we are righteous or even right. It does not even prove that we have *understood* correctly what He said. The infallibility of the messenger and the message does not guarantee the infallibility of our reception.

Now this is an especially important point to make, since the appeal to "God told me," or "the Lord led me," is commonly used to prove that *I* am right, or that *you* should follow *me,* or that *I* should get *my* way. No such claim is justified. But this is such a common misunderstanding of divine guidance that some may say, What is the use of it then? Why should God speak to me or I listen if it will not give me authority and absolutely ensure that I am on the right track?

In the chapters which follow I hope to give some satisfactory response to this question. We shall in due order have to examine the entire issue of authority and *being right* in relation to divine guidance. What must be constantly kept before us in our efforts to comprehend what guidance is and how it works, however, is that God's purposes in guidance are not merely to secure and support us in our various roles or to make sure that *we* are right.

Indeed, being right is one of the hardest burdens human beings have to bear, and few succeed in bearing up under it gracefully. There is a little placard I have seen which reads: "Lord, when we are wrong, make us willing to change, and when we are right make us easy to live with!" A very wise prayer. Paul the apostle has warned us that knowledge puffs up, while love builds up, and that no one knows anything as well as he ought to know it (1 Cor. 8:1-2). The guidance which we seek in the way of Christ is only one part of a life of humility, power, faith, and hopeful love whose final overall character is *life with God* in the embrace of "the everlasting arms" (Deut. 33:27).

Our next chapter must give us a clearer picture of what the experience of that life is like, of how it is that we are to be *with God.*

Questions

1. What are the three general guidelines to guidance which are presented in this chapter?

2. Is your view of "God's will" much different than the "Stepford wives' story"? Why is that stereotype so easy to fall into? How can it be prevented?

3. What is the relationship between (a) communion (b) conversation (c) guidance?

4. What is "Bible roulette"? Is such a "game" biblical?

5. Just because a person is the recipient of communication/guidance from God doesn't make that person infallible, better or right, even about religious matters. Discuss.

6. What is "humble arrogance"? How do we get trapped in it? How can we get out?

7. "Love is a way of 'being with' someone." Discuss.

8. What is true "meekness" according to A. T. Pierson? How is it related to guidance? to the "problem of success"?

9. What is the basic "context" within which guidance occurs?

10. What is wrong with the typical concept of God-as-taskmaster?

Notes

1. The Council of Chalcedon (451 A.D.) makes this use of the idea of Virgin Birth: "That Christ was really divine and really human; in his divinity co-eternal, and in all points similar to the Father; in his humanity, son of the Virgin Mary, *born like all others,* and like unto us men in all things except sin." (Quoted—the emphasis added—from p. 509 of the article on Monophysites in McClintock and Strong, edd., *Cyclopaedia of Biblical, Theological and Ecclesiastical Literature,* New York: Harper and Row, Publishers, 1894.)

2. A. W. Tozer, *The Root of the Righteous* (Harrisburg, PA: Christian Publications, 1955), p. 34.

3. A. T. Pierson, *George Müeller of Bristol and His Witness to a Prayer-Hearing God* (New York: Baker and Taylor Co., 1899), pp. 185-186.

CHAPTER 3

NEVER ALONE

And the Lord God said, It is not good that the man should be alone (Genesis 2:18).

Behold, a virgin will be with child and bear a son, and she will call his name "Immanuel", that is, "God is with us" (Isaiah 7:14).

And, lo, I am with you alway, even unto the end of the world. Amen (Matthew 28:20).

A little group from the college which I attended as a young man used to go on Thursday evenings to hold religious services for the inmates at a county workhouse located about thirty miles east of Chattanooga, Tennessee. The people imprisoned there were not hardened criminals, but quite ordinary men who were serving short sentences of several months to a year for minor offenses. Isolation from their friends and families caused them to suffer acutely.

They seemed for the most part to really look forward to our weekly visits, but I suspect it was more for the singing than anything else. In our group was a young lady who was a beautiful Christian as well as a fine musician. She would play the accordion and the men would enthusiastically join in the songs and hymns. There was one song in particular which they rarely if ever failed to request:

> I've seen the lightning flashing,
>   I've heard the thunder roll;
> I've felt sin's breakers dashing,
>   Trying to conquer my soul.
> I've heard the voice of Jesus,
>   Telling me still to fight on.
> He promised never to leave me,
>   Never to leave me alone.

Then they would swing into the chorus with all the pathos of desperate men contemplating their last hope on earth:

> No, never alone; no, never alone!
>   He promised never to leave me,
> Never to leave me alone.

I once found myself in London with several days on my hands while waiting for a charter flight back to the United States. A great deal of my time was spent in Westminster Cathedral in meditation and prayer. Not Westminster *Abbey*. In the Abbey one senses the great past—the majestic history of the English people and of God's dealings with them. In the cathedral, by contrast, which is several blocks up from the Abbey toward Victoria Station, I sense a divine presence beyond all national histories. Something about the vast, obscure interior of that building impresses me with the nearness of God.

In front of the cathedral is a square with benches, some tables, and off to one side a religious bookstore and a McDonald's—golden arches and all. Here street people of London come to sleep safely in the morning sun if it is shining, and to glean scraps of *haute cuisine* left by those who dine with McDonald.

I recall watching one woman in particular, on a number of occasions, as she slept—with children and pigeons flocking around her. She was blonde, a little heavyset, and about middle-aged. While she showed the marks of street life, she also looked very much like many a housewife at the center of a happy family. And I thought: "Whose daughter is she? Whose sister, or mother, or neighbor, or classmate? And here she is, alone, alone, alone!"

A similar feeling, but even more profound, had come over me when our first child was born. I painfully realized that this incredibly beautiful little creature which we had brought into the world was utterly separate from me, and that there was nothing *I* could do which would shelter him from his aloneness before time, brutal events, the meanness of other human beings, his own wrong choices, the decay of his own body, and, finally, death.

It simply is not within human capability to care effectively for others in the depths of their life and being, or even to be *with* them—no matter how much we may care *about* them. If we could only be with them, that would *almost* be enough, we think. But we cannot, at least in a way which would satisfy us. For all of us it is true: "You must go there by yourself."

And that would be the last word on the subject, but for God. He *is* able so to penetrate and intertwine Himself within the fibers of the human self that those who are enveloped in His loving companionship need never be alone. This is the meaning of the great affirmations at the end of *Romans* chapter 8: "Who shall separate us from the love of Christ? shall tribulation, or distress, or persecution, or famine, or nakedness, or peril, or sword? . . . .

Nay, in all these things we are more than conquerors through him that loved us. For I am persuaded, that neither death, nor life, nor angels, nor principalities, nor powers, nor things present, nor things to come, nor height, nor depth, nor any other creature, shall be able to separate us from the love of God, which is in Christ Jesus our Lord" (vv. 35, 37-39).

Even our anguish over those dear to us can be completely put to rest when we see them enter this presence from which nothing can separate. The final and complete blessing and ultimate good of man comes to those in The Way of Christ. It is life in the presence of God. The completely adequate word of faith in all our sorrows and all our joy is "Immanuel, God is with us!" Thus we sing:

> Where'er Thou art may we remain;
>   Where'er Thou goest may we go;
> With Thee, O Lord, no grief is pain,
>   Away from Thee all joy is woe.
>
> Oh, may we in each holy tide,
>   Each solemn season, dwell with Thee!
> Content if only by Thy side
>   In life or death we still may be.[1]

"In thy presence," the psalmist says, "is fulness of joy; at thy right hand there are pleasures for evermore" (16:11). Even the valley of the shadow of death is nothing to fear, "for thou art with me" (23:4).

And on the other hand, the fact that God alone can by His presence take away our aloneness explains why the ultimate suffering and punishment is to be separated from the presence of God. The psalmist cries out in terror: "Cast me not away from thy presence; and take not thy holy spirit from me" (51:11). Hell itself, whatever else may be involved, essentially consists in separation from God, made even more unbearable by the never ceasing realization that *we* chose it by our preferred course of life.

It is of course true that the person and presence of God with us is sought in part for its external effects. In many of the world religions the favor of the gods is mainly, or totally, sought because of the advantage it brings. The psalmist, once again, describes the presence of God as a place to hide from the pride of man (31:20; and see 32:7; 27:5). After refusing to enrich and fortify himself with plunder from his victory over the kings (Gen. 14:22-24), Abraham, father of the faithful, is given a vision of God saying to him: "Fear not, . . . I am thy shield, and thy exceeding great reward" (Gen. 15:1). When Jehovah was angered by the sins of the Israelites in their journey to Canaan and seemed about to desert them, Moses prevailed upon Him by saying, "For how then can it be known that I have found favor in Thy sight, I and Thy people? Is it not by Thy going with us, so that we, I and Thy people, may be distinguished from all the other people who are upon the face of the earth?" (Exod. 33:16, *NASB*).

Yet the control of our circumstances by means of the presence of God is not, finally, what we rest in as disciples of Jesus. We are instructed to "be content with such things as ye have: for he hath said, 'I will never leave thee nor forsake thee.' So that we may boldly say, The Lord is my helper, and I will not fear what man shall do unto me" (Heb. 13:5-6). The promise here is *not,* however, that God will never allow any evil to come to us, but that no matter what befalls us, we are *still* beyond harm because He is still with us and because His presence is utterly enough *by itself.*

Our contentment lies not in His *presents* but in the *presence* of His person whose presents they are. In all our trials we are more than conquerors *because* nothing "shall be able to separate us from the love of God which is in Christ Jesus our Lord." Good Thomas á Kempis speaks for the ages when he says: "A wise lover regards not so much the gift of Him who loves, as the love of Him who gives. He esteems affection rather than valuables, and sets all gifts below the Beloved. A noble-minded lover rests not in the gift, but in Me above every gift."[2]

We turn to A. W. Tozer again for his statement on the contemporary need in this connection:

> What we need very badly these days is a company of Christians who are prepared to trust God as completely now as they know they must do at the last day. For each of us the time is coming when we shall have nothing but God. Health and wealth and friends and hiding places will be swept away and we shall have only God. To the man of pseudo faith that is a terrifying thought, but to real faith it is one of the most comforting thoughts the heart can entertain.[3]

The sustenance of the Presence Beloved has, through the ages, incidentally made the sickbed sweet and the graveside triumphant, transformed broken hearts and relations, brought glory to drudgery, poverty, and old age, and has turned the martyr's stake or noose into a place of coronation. And when we come to our final home, as Saint Augustine has written, "There we shall rest and see, see and love, love and praise. This is what shall be in the end without end." It is this for which the soul of man was made. It is his temporal and eternal calling. "Man's chief end is to glorify God and enjoy Him forever."[4]

But now loneliness is loose upon the landscape, haunts the penthouse and the rectory, the executive suite and the governor's mansion, as well as the barren apartment, the assembly line, the cocktail lounge, and the city streets. It is, as Mother Theresa of Calcutta has said, the leprosy of the modern world. The popular song of some years back deplored the fate of Eleanor Rigby and exclaimed: "All the lonely people! Where do they all come from?" There is a simple and correct answer to this question. The lonely people live apart from God. They have "no hope, and [are] without God in the world" (Eph. 2:12). Their manifold other alienations are rooted in their alienation from God.

Is it possible to make clear what life *with God* is like, that life wherein one is *never alone*? Can we at least set it forth in terms which would enable the honest and open-minded person to approach the possibility of entering into it? We shall attempt to do this by discussing various forms which God's presence with us may take.

The Dark Night of the Soul

"And ye shall be unto me a kingdom of priests, and an holy nation" (Exod. 19:6).

"Unto him that loved us, and washed us from our sins in his own blood, and hath made us kings and priests unto God and his Father; to him be glory and dominion for ever and ever" (Rev. 1:5-6).

We are, then, looking for a concrete way of understanding our relationship to God. The words just quoted give us some indication of the form which our being with God is to take. There is a great need to clear up this matter, for if we do not we may think of God's presence only as an object of blind faith or abstract reasoning, with no indication and no awareness of Him *really* being there for us at all.

Such a "blind" faith is not to be despised. It is often appropriate even in the life of the devout believer and serves an essential function in bringing the children of God to maturity. There is even a special name for it, "the dark night of the soul," which for centuries has been used in penetrating discussions of the spiritual life.[5] But the reason why this kind of faith stands out so clearly and is thought to be "dark" is precisely its strong contrast with *other* times when God is encountered as "our refuge and strength, a very present help in trouble" (Ps. 46:1).

The heart can never be content to treat God's being with us *merely* as a matter of blind faith, with nothing else to go on. Abstract reasoning from the doctrine of God's omnipresence, or mental assent to the dogma that God *must* be with the believer, are not the primary forms in which God is with us. Those who understand His presence in this way alone must be encouraged to believe that there is much more for them to know. Otherwise they will never enter into their capacity as kings and priests, never "reign in life by one, Jesus Christ" (Rom. 5:17).

Sensing God's Presence

Perhaps the first step beyond mere faith that God *must* be here is an indeterminate but often very powerful sense or feeling or impression of God's presence. Much—as we shall later see—like our experience of the *voice* of God, considerable experience is required to recognize accurately and assess the meanings of such impressions. Yet a sense of God's presence frequently finds its verification in the judgment of the worshiping community, serving as a basis for intelligent appraisal and cooperation by and between individual members of the group. Different people simultaneously sense that given things are to be done: that *God* is moving in that direction.

Experienced ministers and laymen are frequently found unerringly to synchronize their activities in a meeting through this "sense" of God's presence and of His intent for the particular occasion. It is something they come to expect and to rely upon.

Those, on the other hand, who sense God's presence while alone in prayer, service, meditation, or study, find easy communication with multitudes of others who have had similar—or even, it often seems, identical—experiences. They talk a common language, based upon the sameness of their individual experiences.

Such a sense of the presence of another also occurs, as we know, at a "purely secular" level where the "other" is a human being. We may have the distinct impression that someone is looking at us or listening to us, and later learn that a particular person was indeed looking intently at us or listening to us at that time. There are those who are able to get the attention of others (across a large lecture hall, for example) merely by intently staring at the back of their heads. Some "smart" weapons of warfare are able to detect when they are being "watched" by radar, and we are not altogether unlike them. Some persons seem more sensitive than others to such things, just as some have better eyesight or more acute hearing than others; but it seems clear enough that the conscious concentration of some person upon us often has the power to evoke our reciprocal awareness of the one who is focused upon us. Since this is known to be true among human beings, we should not be surprised that *God's* attention to us should result in a reciprocal awareness of His presence.

The God Who Acts

The sense of God's presence is sometimes accompanied in Christian experience by extraordinary events or powerful effects not easily attributable, if at all, to natural causes. This range of effects is a third form taken by God's presence with us, and the sense of presence is by no means essential to it. One of the functions of the "dark night of the soul," referred to above, is to train us to act in reliance upon God, and to cooperate with His working when we *feel* as though we are acting alone. To be able so to act is absolutely necessary if we are to live as if we were independent agents in harmony with the workings of God's Kingdom. Beyond the maturation of our own souls as co-laborers with God, the crucial thing in our service with His Kingdom is the work done; and the mark of the working of God's Spirit with us is always the *incommensurability* of the effects with our merely human powers. These effects also conform to the principles and purposes of the rule of God in human history as manifested in Christ and the Scriptures.

After many years of highly successful ministry, Dwight

Lyman Moody had an experience of which he himself said:

> I cannot describe it, I seldom refer to it, it is almost too sacred an experience to name. . . . I can only say God revealed Himself to me, and I had such an experience of His love that I had to ask Him to stay His hand. I went to preaching again. The sermons were not different; I did not present any new truths; and yet hundreds were converted. I would not now be placed back where I was before that blessed experience if you should give me all the world; it would be as small dust in the balance.[6]

In his day, Moody was a constant source of wonder precisely because "his" effects were so totally incommensurable with his obvious personal qualities. He was a man of very ordinary appearance, unordained by any ecclesiastical group, and quite uncultured and uneducated—even uncouth and crude to many. At the height of Moody's effectiveness, in 1874-1875, Dr. R. W. Dale, one of the leading nonconformist clergymen in England, observed his work for three or four days in Birmingham. He wished to discover the secret of Moody's power. After his observation he told Moody that the work was most plainly the work of God, for he could see no relation between him personally and what he was accomplishing. A smaller person might well have been offended at this, but Moody only laughed and replied that he would be very sorry if things were otherwise.[7]

We recall the biblical story of how Abraham fathered Isaac—the son of promise and spirit—upon Sarah, contrary to nature, through the energy of the Spirit. But Ishmael was begotten upon Hagar quite naturally through the mere energies of the flesh (Gal. 4:22-28). Life with effects beyond the natural always depends upon intimate interchange between us and God who is *present*.

When Paul and Barnabas went forth on their first missionary journey (Acts 13–14) they moved at every turn in a power that was far beyond themselves. The result was an astonishing series of events, establishing communities of believers in Christ throughout central Asia Minor. When they returned to their home in Syrian Antioch they brought the community of believers together and matter-of-factly "rehearsed all that God had done *with them,* and how *he* had opened the door of faith unto the Gentiles" (Acts 14:27, italics added). There was no doubt of God's presence with them because it was He who energized their activities with a power beyond themselves. The fulfillment of Jesus' words concerning the divine helper—"He dwelleth with you, and shall be in you" (John 14:17)—was to them the most obvious fact of their lives. "He that raised up Christ from the dead" also quickened *their* mortal bodies by His Spirit which dwelt within them (Rom. 8:11; also Eph. 1:19-20).

We have now considered three forms or aspects of God's presence with us: when He *is* indeed close to us, but remains unevidenced in any way, being the object of "blind" faith or abstract reasoning; when He is *sensed,* or there is a strong impression of His presence; and when He *acts* in conjunction with our actions to change our surroundings in ways beyond our own powers.

"I make it my business to persevere in His Holy presence, wherein I keep myself by a simple attention, and a general fond regard to God, which I may call an *actual presence* of God; or, to speak better, an habitual, silent, and secret conversation of the soul with God, which often causes me joys and raptures inwardly, and sometimes also outwardly, so great that I am forced to use means to moderate them and prevent their appearance to others" (Brother Lawrence).

Many who agree with what I have written in the preceding pages might wish to stop at this point and accept what we have thus far discussed as a complete account of the forms of God's presence. But I believe that to stop now would be to omit what is most important in the ongoing relationship between man and God, and to rob the idea of the priesthood and royalty of the believer of its substance. It would leave our interaction with God too close to the level of vague feelings, the Ouija board, and even superstitious conjecture. How shall we reign in life by Christ Jesus on such a basis? How can we be *friends* of God if this is all there is to it? How is the rich conceptual content and knowledge found in the Bible to be understood as something communicated to man if the three forms of presence thus far discussed is the totality of man's interaction with God? Why, if God be personal, would He not also *talk* with us?

God's Presence As Conversational Relationship

Thus we must add to the above that God is also with us in a conversational relationship: that He *speaks* with us individually as it is appropriate—as is common between persons who know one another, care about each other, and are engaged in common enterprises. It is just such a conversational manner of presence which is suited to that *personal* relationship with God that is so often spoken of in the community of believers. It is this which turns Paul's statement, "As many as are led by the Spirit of God are the children of God" (see Rom. 8:14) into a framework for *personal* development, as distinct from incitement to play the robot or a reader of vague impressions and signs.

Now there are, as is generally understood, two types of guidance commonly found in human experience. One is that *mechanical* variety which we see in driving an automobile or in the "remote" electronic control of a model airplane or space probe. We guide anything when by conscious effort and means we cause it to proceed in a certain way, and the simplest and clearest cases fall within this area of mechanical guidance.

But there is also personal guidance. Here too we wish

to bring events to proceed in a certain way, but we are dealing with *people,* and they have a *mind* with which to consider matters on their own, and a *will* concerning what is to be done. The ideal, then, for *personal* guidance is to bring things to the desired outcome but, at the same time, to give the *mind* guided its fullest scope and the *will* its uncoerced play. Thus the outcome really is the work of the individual guided, not merely of the one who is guiding. It remains his or her life after all, since we have "guided" them only through their own understanding, deliberation, and decision. For this purpose we must *communicate* with the one who is to be guided. Only this provides a mode of personal interaction which permits us to impact persons guided in a way that makes a difference and yet leaves them the mental space to retain their integrity as free personalities, to live as our friends and govern their own lives.

Now God generally deals with His nonhuman or nonpersonal creation as one guides an automobile: by a causal influence mediated through the general system of physical reality that He has ordained in His creation. Job is asked whether he, like God, "can . . . lead forth a constellation in its season, and guide the Bear with her satellites" (Job 38:32, *NASB*). But God's personal creatures, whether angelic or human, are guided by *communication* of His intentions and thoughts. They are *addressed* by Him. We are admonished in Psalm 32:9: "Do not be as the horse or as the mule which have no *understanding,* whose harness includes bit and bridle to keep them in check." We are to be led by—guided by—reasonable, intelligible communication, not by blind impulse, force or sensation.

Guidance by Words

But such a communication may occur in one of two ways. First, *through what we will recognize as a voice,* or as *words* addressed to—or even through—us. If one takes this type of communication away, the biblical experience of

God's presence is simply wiped out. The primary manner of communication from God to man is the Word of God, or God speaking, and the Bible itself remains to us as God's Word written down. God spoke directly to Moses, to Ezekiel, to Paul, and to many others; and then through them indirectly to the people of Israel, to the Church, and now—in the Bible—to world history.

In Acts 9:10-16, for example, we have the story of a man named Ananias. The events here immediately follow the time in which Paul was struck down when the risen Christ addressed him on the road to Damascus. Paul went into seclusion in Damascus and was fasting and in prayer for three days. Apparently about the end of that period of time, the Lord appeared to his fellow believer Ananias, of the same city, and told him that he should go and speak to Paul (then Saul). Thus Paul was put in touch with and ministered to by the believers in Damascus.

What we see here is not a matter of abstract argumentation, of vague impressions, or of naturally unaccountable events. The same is true for Peter's experience on the rooftop in Joppa (Acts 10) before being called to preach the gospel in the house of Cornelius, the Roman.

Such things happened to Paul over and over. He was about to go into Bithynia, for example, on his second missionary journey; and somehow, as we are told in Acts 16:6-9, the Holy Spirit would not let him go. Then, as he waited at Troy, he had a dream that he should, instead of staying on his home territory in Asia Minor, take a radically new direction and enter into Europe; a dream of a man of Macedonia saying, "Come over and help us."

These purposeful and conscious communications by words seem to have been quite normal experiences for the early Christians. If we look at the advice on how the meetings of the Church were supposed to proceed as given in 1 Corinthians 14, we see that it is assumed that numerous people in the congregation are going to have some kind of communication from God which they will be sharing with the others in the group. "What is the outcome then, brethren? When you assemble, each one has a psalm, has a teaching, has a revelation, has a tongue, has an interpretation" (14:26, *NASB*).

The prophecy of Joel fulfilled in the early Church was: "Your sons and daughters shall prophesy, and your young men shall see visions, and your old men shall dream dreams" (Acts 2:17, *NASB*; Joel 2:28-32). The wish of Moses "that all the Lord's people were prophets, and that the Lord would put his spirit upon them" (Num. 11:29) is then substantially granted in the Church of Jesus Christ functioning as intended by its Lord.

Guidance by Shared Activity

Second, there is still another way in which intentions and thoughts of God are communicated to those who are with Him. One which involves a much more *active* role on the part of the recipient. It is a way very common to those who are most mature in His family or Kingdom, for here we come to understand what God wants us to understand because we are engaged and immersed in His work with Him and understand what He is doing so well that we know what He is thinking and intending to do. I believe that this is a great part of the condition described by Paul the apostle as *having the mind of Christ:* "He who is spiritual appraises all things, yet he himself is appraised of by no man. For who has known the mind of the Lord, that he should instruct Him? But we have the mind of Christ" (1 Cor. 2:15-16, *NASB*).

There is an interesting statement in relation to this way of being with God in Psalm 32. The psalmist here says (in the King James Version), "I will instruct thee and teach thee in the way which thou shalt go: I will guide thee with mine eye" (v. 8). Newer versions generally say: "I will guide you with my eye *upon* you." But there are two very clear and distinct types of experiences where one person is guided *by* the eye of another. First, there are very few husbands, wives, or children who have not upon occasion been forcibly guided by being looked *at* by their mate or parent. The fatherly or motherly eye upon the child speaks silent volumes of profound instruction upon a moment's notice.

But there is yet another and even more important way in which we are guided by the eye of another. This is when we are working or playing closely with them and know the intents and thoughts of their mind by our awareness of what they are focused upon. Someone can effectively work with me only if they can see what I am doing and not have to be *told* what I am thinking and what they should do to be of help. The model employee, for example, is by no means someone who stands waiting, no matter how solicitously, for someone to tell him what to do; and everyone breathes easier when the new person on the job no longer has to be told.

There is a similar distinction to be drawn with respect to levels of friendship. In *The Transforming Friendship,* Leslie Weatherhead describes a kind of friendship that is beyond words. He asks:

> If my friend's mother in a distant town falls ill and he urgently desires to visit her, which would reveal deeper friendship—my lending him my motor-bike in response to his request for it, or my taking it to his door for him as soon as I heard of the need, without waiting to be asked? In the first case there has to be a request made with a voice. But in the second the fact of the friendship creates in me a longing to help. The first illustrates the communion between two persons on what we might call the level of the seen; but the second illustrates the communion, at a deeper level, of two persons on what we may call the level of the unseen.[8]

In many cases our need to wonder about, or be told, what God wants in a certain situation is a clear indication of how little we are engaged in His work. On one sabbath Jesus found a man with a withered hand in the synagogue (Mark 3:1-5). He called him forth and asked the good people gathered about whether or not one should do good on the sabbath (heal the man) or do evil (leave him in distress). The whole condition of these people was loudly and eloquently declared by their silence. They did not know what to do! "They held their peace." After He had healed the man, however, they thought it right to lay plans to kill Jesus. This was only another fruit of the same heart which could *wonder* whether or not the man should be healed. But Jesus knew what God wanted done in this case because He knew the mind of God generally. On another occasion where He was denounced for healing on the sabbath He calmly replied: "My Father worketh hitherto, and I work" (John 5:17).

If we are right, then, our union with God—His presence with us in which our aloneness is banished and the meaning and full purpose of human existence is realized—consists chiefly in a conversational relationship between God and the individual soul who is consistently and deeply engaged as His friend and co-laborer in the Kingdom of God. There is a place for "blind" faith in God's presence as well as for the "feeling" or sense that He is there and the supernatural effects of His presence. But no amount of these can take the place of intelligible communication through word and shared activity.[9]

When *all* of these types of presence are in place, it is then that the royal priesthood of the believer is realized as it should be. It is then that having a "personal relationship" with God becomes a concrete and commonsense reality rather than a nervous whistling in the spiritual dark. God indeed does guide us in many ways by special acts of intervention in our lives as well as by general providential ordering of the world. But His direct communication with us, by word and by shared activity, is the most important part of His guidance because it calls forth to full development that in us which is most in His image: our understanding, our values, and our will.

Human personality on the Christian viewpoint is an incarnate system of mental and physical acts designed to be inhabited by God. We are to be the temple of God, but one which actively understands and cooperates with God's purposes and is inhabited through a willing, clear-eyed identification of ourselves with God, enabled by God Himself. Thus, Christ *in us* is our hope of glory (Col. 1:27). Thus, "I am crucified with Christ: nevertheless I live; yet not I, but Christ liveth in me: and the life which I now live in the flesh I live by the faith of the Son of God, who loved me, and gave himself for me" (Gal. 2:20).

In concluding this chapter it may be useful, as a clarification of what has been said, to single out three positions which are commonly taken but which seem to be mistaken and very harmful to the search for guidance.

Message-a-Minute

There is, first, *the Message-A-Minute view.* On this view God is either telling you what to do at every turn of the road, or He is willing and available to tell you if you only would ask Him.

Now I do not believe that either the Bible or our shared experience in The Way of Christ will bear out this view. There is no evidence in the life of Paul, for example, that he was constantly receiving communications from God. The union which Christ had with the Father was the greatest that we can conceive of in this life. Yet there is no indication that He was constantly awash with revelations as to what He should do. His union with the Father was so great that He was at all times obedient; and yet this obedience was something that rested in His mature will and understanding of His life before God, *not* on always being told, "Now do this," and "Now do that."

Putting it this way returns us to our theme that divine guidance is ultimately for the mature personality. This is not to say that people upon conversion, or as they first enter the Church or begin to come alive in their experience of God, do not have guidance. God meets us where we are. Yet the *aim* of God in working through the Holy Spirit and the indwelling Christ to guide us is not to keep us constantly under His dictation. Too much intrusion upon a seed that has been planted, or a plant, or a child, simply makes normal, healthy growth impossible.

Thus, E. Stanley Jones writes:

> I believe in miracle, but not too much miracle, for too much miracle would weaken us, make us dependent on miracle instead of our obedience to natural law. Just enough miracle to let us know He is there, but not too much, lest we depend on it when we should depend on our own initiative and on His orderly processes for our development.[10]

The redemptive community will not consist of robots but of mature people who know how to live together and who know how to live with God. And for that reason, I think this model of a message-a-minute to be mistaken and very harmful in our search for guidance. Of course the question is not whether God *could* give a message each minute. Surely He could give that, and more, if it would suit His purpose of bringing forth the cosmic family of God. But it does not.

This is something we must remember as we develop our educational programs, hold our evangelistic meetings and teaching missions, and carry on with all of the activities of the church. In our services and in our models of the ministry and of ministers, we must remember that we are not making robots who sing, clap, pray, give, and show up for meetings when they are supposed to. We are bringing forth the sons and daughters of God to live in this world to His glory. We must suit our means to *that* end.

It's-All-in-the-Bible

The second view of guidance which I take the liberty of calling misguided is *the It's-All-in-the-Bible view.* Here we have a view which tries to honor the Bible, but with a zeal which is not according to knowledge. About many questions in our lives the Bible gives direct instructions. We do not need to make long inquiries into God's will in order to know whether we should worship an idol or mistreat our parents. But many other questions force us to realize that *we* and the specific circumstances of our lives are simply not dealt with in the Bible.

The Bible will not tell which song you are supposed to sing next Sunday, or which verse you should take as a text for a talk or a sermon. Yet it is very likely that God's leading is claimed for nothing more frequently than for the selection of texts and sermon topics. The Bible will not tell you what to do with most of the details of your life. You want to know how to raise your children? It will tell you some very important things, but not everything you need and want to know on that subject. Your family, your work, your community will face you with many, many choices and issues that the Bible simply says nothing specific about. The *principles* are all there. I would happily agree that in principle the Bible says all that needs to be said. But the principles have to be applied before they can be lived out. And it is largely at the point of application that almost everything that we can imagine has been "proven" from the Bible. This is in part because the principles of "proof" have to be scandalously loosened before one can get the "applications" so desperately desired.

Our reverence for and faith in the Bible must not be allowed to blind us to the need for personal divine guidance within the principles of the Bible, but beyond the details of what it explicitly says. A distinguished minister recently said on a nationally televised program that if we would only accept the Bible as the Word of God, all differences between Christians would be resolved. But in fact it is Bible-believing Christians who disagree with each other most often and most heatedly. Nearly every faction in Christendom claims the Bible as its basis, but then disagrees as to what the Bible says. An exalted view of the Bible does not free us from the responsibility of learning to talk with God and hear Him in the many ways He speaks to us.

It is a misguided expectation of the Bible with reference to individual guidance that leads some people to play the game of "Bible roulette." They allow the Bible to fall open where it will and then stab their finger at random on the page to see which verse it lands on. Then they read the verse thus lighted upon to see what they should do. I believe that God does *use* this method, though I think He does not *choose* it. It is an ancient practice followed on some occasions by many great Christians such as Saint Augustine and Saint Francis of Assisi.

In the thirty-second year of his life, Augustine was under deep conviction after long prayer by his mother, Monica, and deep searching by the Holy Spirit. Half delirious from his agony of mind, he wandered in a garden,

> . . . speaking [to God] and weeping in the most bitter contrition of my heart, when, lo! I heard from a neighbouring house a voice, as of boy or girl, I know not, chanting, and oft repeating, "Take up and read; Take up and read." Instantly, my countenance altered, I began to think most intently, whether children were wont in any kind of play to sing such words; nor could I remember ever to have heard the like. So, checking the torrent of my tears, I arose; interpreting it to be no other than a command

> from God to open the book, and read the first chapter I should find. For I had heard of Antony, that coming in during the reading of the Gospel, he received the admonition, as if what was being read, was spoken to him: *Go, sell all that thou hast, and give to the poor, and thou shalt have treasure in heaven, and come and follow me:* and by such oracle he was forthwith converted unto Thee. Eagerly then I returned to the place where . . . I had laid the volume of the Apostle when I arose thence. I seized, opened, and in silence read that section on which my eyes first fell: *Not in rioting and drunkenness, not in chambering and wontonness, not in strife and envying: but put ye on the Lord Jesus Christ, and make not provision for the flesh,* in concupiscense. No further would I read; nor needed I: for instantly at the end of this sentence, by a light as it were of serenity infused into my heart, all the darkness of doubt vanished away [11]

Of the practice of Saint Francis, G. K. Chesterton writes:

> It seems almost the opposite of searching the Scriptures to open them at random; but St. Francis certainly opened them at random. According to one story, he merely made the sign of the cross over the volume of the Gospel and opened it at three places, reading three texts. The first was the tale of the rich young man whose refusal to sell all his goods was the occasion of the great paradox about the camel and the needle. The second was the commandment to the disciples to take nothing with them in their journey, neither scrip nor staff nor any

> money. The third was that saying, literally to be called crucial, that the follower of Christ must also carry his cross.[12]

In spite of the greatness of some of its users, this certainly is not a procedure recommended in the Bible, and there is no *biblical* reason why one might not just as well use the dictionary or the *Encyclopedia Brittanica* or the morning newspaper, or why one might not as well open the Bible and wait for a fly to land upon a verse.

A novel approach was recently suggested by a minister who stated in all seriousness that we should look up the year of our birth to cast light upon what we should do. Unless you were born in the first half of this century, and the earlier the better, this method will do you no good, since there are few verses numbered beyond 20 or 30. I was born in 1935, so I thought I would see what direction I could get from Genesis 19:35. I will leave it to your curiosity to see what that verse says, but one shudders to think what "guidance" might be derived from this method.

Now, of course, God is so great that He can use almost anything for His purposes in the life of one sincerely seeking Him. Even truly superstitious methods are not beyond His forbearance and use. In the upper room (Acts 1:26) lots were cast—something like flipping a coin or drawing straws—to determine who would replace Judas among the twelve apostles. This method was often used in biblical times, and Proverbs 16:33 *(NKJV)* assures us that while the lot is cast into the lap, "its every decision is from the Lord." However, even the most biblically oriented churches of today would not think of rolling dice or flipping a coin to determine policy for the church or settle an issue in some individual member's life. This is true even though all might agree that God *could* determine the coin or the dice to come out as He wished.

We have made some progress. Nevertheless, you still hear people tell of opening the Bible at random and reading a random verse to decide whether to undertake some enterprise or move or marry a certain person. Many devout persons will do such things to get "guidance"—so great is their need and anxiety, though they may later try to hide it or laugh at it when revealed. Worse still, many actually act upon their "guidance" to the great harm of themselves and others about them. They are the losers at "Bible roulette."

What a stark contrast to this unhappy condition is the simple word of Jesus: "My sheep hear my voice, and I know them, and they follow me" (John 10:27).

Whatever-Comes

A third mistaken view of guidance is *the Whatever-Comes view.* This is very commonly adopted and has much to recommend it in terms of the peace of mind and freedom from struggle which it provides. But, in fact, it amounts to giving up any possibility of guidance as a conscious interchange between God and His children. The view even shows up in some of our most loved hymns. There is a well-known hymn titled, "If Thou But Suffer God to Guide Thee." This may seem to be exactly what we are talking about: allowing God to guide us. But when we study the hymn closely we find that there is in it a council to accept *everything* that happens to us as the guidance of God.

Now I do not like to criticize this view because, as I have already acknowledged, there is so much practical good in its effects, when sincerely accepted. But on the other hand I have talked to far too many devout Christians who are tremendously puzzled because they cannot make any sense out of prayer, out of choices—and many times very hard choices—as to what *they* are *to do,* using the view that whatever comes is God's guidance. If you wish to know what God would have *you* do, it is no help at all to be told that whatever comes is His will. For you are, precisely, in the position of having to decide in some measure what *is* to come. Does it mean that whatever you do will be God's will? Certainly not.

We can at least say that if Moses had accepted this view there would have been no nation of Israel. Perhaps a nation of "Mosesites" instead. When the people made and worshiped the golden calf while Moses was on Sinai receiving God's commandments, God said: "I will destroy them, and make of thee [Moses] a great nation" (Exod. 32:10). Moses not only did not accept "whatever comes," he actually and successfully withstood God's own declared intent in the matter, appealing to God's reputation before the surrounding nations and to his friendship with Abraham. "And the Lord repented of the evil which he thought to do unto his people" (Exod. 32:14).

Many things that happen are not the will of God, although obviously He does not act to stop them. "It is not the will of God that any should perish, but that all should come to repentance" (2 Pet. 3:9). But nevertheless people *do* perish and fail to come to repentance.

God's world is an arena in which we have an indispensable role to play. The issue is not simply, "What does God want?" but also, "What do we want and will?" To accept whatever comes is not guidance. Merely that something happens does not indicate that it is God's will. Throughout much of our lives God's will is that *we* should determine what will happen. What the child does when not told what to do is the final indicator of what and who that child is. And so it is for us and our heavenly Father. We shall return to this point in our last chapter.

Against these three mistaken views of divine guidance we set a conversational view where—in a manner to be further explored in pages to follow—there is appropriate, clear, specific communication through conscious experience from God to the individual believer within the context of a life immersed in God's kingdom.

"Then shalt thou call, and the Lord shall

> answer; thou shalt cry, and he shall say, Here I am . . . . And the Lord shall guide thee continually, and satisfy thy soul in drought, and make fat thy bones: and thou shalt be like a watered garden, and like a spring of water, whose waters fail not" (Isa. 58:9,11).

But there are many who will wonder if we really do live in a universe where this could happen. Does the human and physical reality of our universe call for it or allow it? This is an issue to which we must now turn.

Questions

1. What does it mean to be "alone" in the universe? Is it possible to be "alone in a crowd"? in a "church"?
2. Does being "never alone" mean that we are immune from the effects of evil? Why?
3. What are the three basic forms of experiencing "God's presence"? What are the benefits/limits of each?
4. What is the Dark Night of the Soul? What can be learned from going through it?
5. How can one "sense" God's presence?
6. How can God "act" in our lives? How can we know it?
7. What are the two general types of "guidance" familiar to human experience?
8. What are the two aspects of "personal" guidance?
9. What is the relationship between God's presence,

communication and guidance?

10. What must one understand and do in order to have a conversational relationship with God?

Notes

1. Anglican hymn.
2. Thomas á Kempis, *The Imitation of Christ* (Chicago: Moody Press, 1958), pp. 106-107.
3. A. W. Tozer, *The Root of Righteousness* (Harrisburg, PA: Christian Publications, 1955).
4. *Westminster Confession of Faith,* "Shorter Catechism," 1st par.
5. St. John of the Cross, *Dark Night of the Soul* (Garden City, NY: Image Books, 1959), pp. 36-39.
6. A. P. Fitt, *The Shorter Life of D. L. Moody* (Chicago: Moody Press, 1900), p. 67.
7. Ibid., p. 76.
8. Leslie Weatherhead, *The Transforming Friendship* (London: Epworth Press, 1962), p. 54.
9. An excellent supplementary discussion to the above is found under the heading, "General Manners of the Divine Presence," in Section III of Chapter 1 of Jeremy Taylor's *The Rule and Excercise of Holy Living,* first published in 1650.
10. E. Stanley Jones, *A Song of Ascents* (Nashville: Abingdon Press, 1979), p. 191.
11. *The Confessions of Saint Augustine,* book 8, par. 29 (italics added).
12. G. K. Chesterton, *St. Francis of Assisi* (New York: Doubleday & Company, Inc., 1957), p. 61.

CHAPTER 4

OUR COMMUNICATING COSMOS

Earth's crammed with Heaven, And every common bush afire with God; But only he who sees takes off his shoes (Elizabeth Barrett Browning).

In him we live, and move, and have our being (Acts 17:28).

We have given a number of stories about God's guidance of well-known Christians—even about them being *spoken* to in various ways. There is a practically endless supply of such stories, and each is of considerable intrinsic interest. I love to dwell upon such stories myself and I have noticed that people rarely tire of hearing them, even if they don't entirely believe them.

Another favorite of mine concerns Peter Marshall, the Scotsman who in the middle years of this century became one of the most widely acclaimed ministers of our times and, by his outstanding qualities as a man and as a minister, gained a new level of prominence for the office of the chaplain of the United States Senate. In a foggy, pitch-black Northumberland night he cut across the moors of his native land in an area where lay a deep, deserted limestone quarry. As he plodded blindly forward, an urgent voice called out, "Peter!" He stopped and answered: "Yes, who is it? What do you want?" But there was no response. Thinking he was mistaken, he took a few more steps. Then again, even more urgently, "Peter! . . . " At this he stopped again and, trying to peer into the darkness, stumbled forward and fell to his knees. Putting down his hand to brace himself, he found nothing there. As he felt around in a semicircle he discovered that he was right on the brink of the abandoned quarry, where one more step certainly would have killed him.[1]

The popular devotional magazine *Guideposts,* edited by Norman Vincent Peale and Ruth Stafford Peale, provides a constant stream of such stories, and the same is true for a large number of other widely read religious papers and magazines from almost every denomination and theological persuasion.

But we have now come to a point in our study where we must recognize that there is a limit to what can be accomplished for the growth of faith by contemplating such stories—no matter how well attested they may be, and no matter how reliable the minds and characters of the people involved. And this limit is not a matter neglected by the teachings of the Bible itself.

According to the story told by Jesus in Luke 16, "a certain rich man" died and found himself tormented in Hades. There he saw poor Lazarus, who used to beg at his gate, afar off from him and at peace in the close company of Abraham. The rich man now saw the error of his ways and wished to keep his five brothers still on earth from joining him in the place of torment. He asked father Abraham to send Lazarus back to tell them of his fate so that they might avoid it. This instructive conversation then follows: "Abraham saith unto him, They have Moses and the prophets; let them hear them. And he said, Nay, father Abraham: but if one went unto them from the dead, they will repent. And [Abraham] said unto them, If they hear not Moses and the prophets, neither will they be persuaded, though one rose from the dead" (Luke 16:29-31).

The Limits of Signs

We also recall from the New Testament record that Jesus refused to do religious stunts or "signs" for those who demanded them (Matt. 12:39-40; Mark 8:11-12; Luke 23:8-9; John 2:18; 6:30). I believe that this was because He knew that such deeds, no matter how wondrous, would be fruitless against the false ideas and minds-set of the observers. We cannot imagine that *He* would have withheld signs if they truly could have helped people to have genuine faith in Him. But they could not. It is precisely our preexisting ideas and assumptions that largely determine what we *can* see, hear, or otherwise observe. They cannot, therefore, be changed by stories and miraculous events only, since they prevent correct perception of such stories and events.

Agnes Sanford, the young wife of an Episcopal minister, relates how her baby had a serious ear infection. It lasted for six weeks while she prayed fearfully and fruitlessly. But a neighboring minister called to see her husband and learned that the baby was sick. He quite casually, though intently and in a businesslike manner, prayed for the baby, which immediately shut its eyes, lost its fever flush, and went to sleep. When it awoke, the fever was gone and its ears were well.

Mrs. Sanford remarks:

> The strange thing is that this did not immediately show me a new world. Instead, it perplexed me greatly. Why did God answer the

> minister's prayers when He had not answered mine? I did not know that I myself blocked my own prayers, because of my lack of faith. Nor did I know that this prayer could not come through me because my mind was clogged with resentment and darkness and unhappiness, as a pipeline can be clogged with roots and dirt. This doubt and confusion remained in my mind, even though the child himself, whenever he subsequently had a bit of an earache, demanded that I pray for him.[2]

But this really is not strange, once we understand how our minds work. It only illustrates the fact that beholding or being told of God's interventions in our lives—whether to guide us, speak to us, or perform saving deeds in our behalf—does not automatically clear up our confusions nor straighten out the entanglements of our hearts. Such events may stimulate us *to seek* faith and understanding, but they do not of themselves *give us* faith and understanding. Our understanding must grow *before* we can have any appreciation of what we are experiencing on those occasions where God intervenes. There must be a prior inward illumination of the mind and spirit, such as came to Peter in his great confession that his friend and acquaintance, Jesus, was in fact the Christ of God (Matt. 16:16-17). This illumination may sometimes come unsought, and it often comes unexpectedly—as seems to have been the case with Peter here. The events immediately following made clear that he did not really understand what he had said concerning Jesus. The insight he gave had slipped up on him.

But God also meets us with inward illumination as we study and as we strive to understand:

> "If you cry out for insight
> and raise your voice for understanding,

if you seek it like silver
  and search for it as for hidden treasures;
then you will understand the fear of the Lord
  and find the knowledge of God" (Prov. 2:3-5, *RSV*).

Now all of this must be kept clearly in view as we go on into the present chapter. Admittedly, we are entering an intellectual and spiritual "hard-hat area." We must deal with a number of difficult problems that trouble many thoughtful Christians and non-Christians alike: problems about the very idea of our being in a conversational relationship with God. If you are one who has no difficulty along these lines, perhaps you should just count your blessings and proceed immediately to chapter 5, which deals with the various ways God uses to personally communicate with man. But if, for whatever reason, you find that you do not have any real confidence that God would or could guide you and speak to you, this chapter may be of some use. Put on your hard hat and your hard nose, and prayerfully dig in.

In fact—and I have verified it in many cases—the honest response of many persons (including many of those who heartily confess and practice faith in Christ) to what has been said in the foregoing chapters will be that God *would not* communicate with run-of-the-mill human beings by surrounding them with His presence and speaking to them, or that He *does not* communicate with *them* in that way, or even that He *cannot* do so. Perhaps yet others, motivated by the need to control the divine presence and word for what they sincerely regard as the proper ends, may even think that God *should* not communicate with individuals as we have indicated He does.

When we are considering whether God *would* be with ordinary human beings in a conversational relationship, we must remember not to conceive of Him in the likeness of human "dignitaries" of our acquaintance. The famous, the rich, and the great among humanity are still severely limited in their powers of communication by the fact that they are *merely* human. The limits of their ability to interact personally with others are very narrow. Therefore, it is possible for them to be in intimate contact with only a small number of other persons—even with all the wonders of modern communications technology. Their span of consciousness, their capacity to pay attention, and the scope of their willpower permits nothing else.

The Lowliness of God

But beyond such factual limitations, human "greatness" is often taken to mean, and essentially requires, having nothing to do with those who are only "ordinary people." It is thought to involve a certain exclusiveness, insularity, or snobbishness. If we are unable to clear our minds of such associations with "greatness," we will be unable to think that the great God would talk to *us*. We will think of Him as a dignitary who is too busy for that, or who is too conscious of His "status," too "high up."

How hard it is for us to come to an adequate conception of the *lowliness* of God and of how it is precisely His greatness which makes Him able, available, and ready to hear and speak personally with the most insignificant of His creatures!

This lowliness was, of course, at the very center of Jesus' teaching about God. In His actions and in His words He made clear the *accessibleness* of God to the weak, to the downtrodden and castaway, to little children. "Suffer little children, and forbid them not, to come unto me: for of such is the kingdom of heaven" (Matt. 19:14). In saying "of such," many interesting characteristics certainly were intended by our Lord, but here we stress the element of "unimportance." The unimportant ones are important to God. God being who He is, and now revealed in the person of Jesus Christ, we should be surprised if He did not speak to us. As E. Stanley Jones has written:

> Does God guide? Strange if he didn't. The Psalmist asks: "He that planted the ear, shall he not hear? He that formed the eyes, shall he not see?" (Ps. 94:9) And I ask: "He that made the tongue and gave us power to communicate with one another, shall he not speak and communicate with us?" I do not believe that God our Father is a dumb, non-communicative impersonality.[3]

But what of those who believe that God just simply and as a matter of fact does not speak to *them*? Here we must consider, I believe, two separate lines along which the cause of their difficulty may be found.

Listening for God

First of all, *that we do not hear does not mean that He is not speaking to us.* It is a very common thing, even at the strictly human level, for us not to hear those who speak to us. It has probably happened to most of us this very day. Someone spoke to us but we did not know it, did not hear it. Moreover, we know now that messages of radio and television programs are passing through our very bodies and brains at all hours of the day: messages which an appropriate receiver appropriately tuned could pluck from the air we breathe. In certain circumstances, the human body can act as an antenna to a radio set. As a child I had a radio set which required me to hold the aerial wire in order to bring in faraway stations. As you now read this, waves bearing a vast number of messages flood around you and even right through you: the evening news, messages from ships at sea, from citizens' band, the police, truck and taxi drivers, possibly even from outer space.

Astronomers who seek for signs of life upon other planets and in other galaxies of our universe say it may well be that earth is being constantly bombarded by messages from outer space, and that we simply don't know how to pick them up, organize them, or recognize their patterns. What an apt picture this is, it seems to me, of the human being in relation to God, showered with messages which simply go right through us or by us. We are not *attuned* to God's voice. We have not been taught how to hear it sounding out in nature—as we read in Psalm 19, "The heavens *declare* the glory of God"—or in a special communication directed by God to the individual mind or soul.

A Ready Vessel?

And this really brings us to our second way of understanding those who say, "God just does not speak to me." Here a bit of honest soul-searching may be required. Possibly they are being spoken to and do not hear. But it may also be that *they could make no good use of a word from God because of how they are living.* Are they ready to obey and change should that be what God directs? It is in general a good thing for God to speak to man. But there may be reasons in the individual case why it would be best for God to speak very little, or even not at all. If it is true that God does not speak to me, then I must inquire whether or not I am such a case.

The question must be asked, To what use would a word from God be put? True, God is not a snob, and He is not far away: "Behold, the Lord's hand is not too short to reach us and save, nor is his ear heavy and unable to hear" (Isa. 59:1). But *when* He speaks it is to accomplish *His* good purposes in our lives and through His creation. Divine guidance is not a gimmick which we can keep on tap for our gain. It is not to enable us to win in our competitions with others. We cannot invoke it to help us win bets on football games or horse races, or to prove that *we* are theologically correct. While it is available to every person who walks with God, it is not *at their disposal* as they see fit without regard to the kingdom of God.

We have already briefly touched upon this point, but it must be hammered home relentlessly. Divine guidance is not for any form of self-aggrandizement. It is not for the enhancement of the ego, for the building up of pride. It is not to prove that "I'm okay." How many times have we heard someone invoke God's support for their cause with a "God says" or a "God told me"—subtly sometimes, sometimes blatantly invoking the voice of God to prove that they are right! But as with all of God's activities in human life, guidance is for the promotion of His kingdom and of our good in that kingdom.

We pray: "Our Father who are in heaven, hallowed be thy name, thy kingdom come, thy will be done on earth as it is in heaven." This preamble to the Lord's prayer beautifully expresses the purpose of all of God's activities in us: "Hallowed be *thy* name. *Thy* kingdom come. *Thy* will be done." Divine guidance—as a reliable, day-to-day reality for people with good sense—is for those who are devoted to the glory of God and the advancement of His kingdom. Guidance is for the disciple of Jesus Christ who has no higher preference than to be like Him. This does not mean that it *never* comes to anyone else. And in the next chapter we will see how God speaks to some very unlikely people. But we have to remember that His mere speaking to someone does not mean that they are right or that they are particularly good. It means only that He wills to communicate to them in order to accomplish His purposes relevant to them.

So if you find yourself in the position of the one who can honestly say, "God has never spoken to me," then you well might ask: "Why *should* God speak to *me*? What am I doing in life that would make His speaking to me a reasonable thing for Him to do?"

When our lives are devoted to the will of God, there is reason for Him to speak to us. If our lives are not devoted to His purposes, then He may still speak to us, use us for His ends. After all, we *are* His creatures, no matter how rebellious. But for a willing walk in conscious, loving cooperation with God, we must come to grips with the issue, *What are we living for?* We must face it *clearly.*

It may well be that I have never come to the place where I can truly say, "I am living for one thing and one thing *only,* and that is to be like Christ and do His work and live among His people and serve them and Him in this world." If we have not come to that place, the question which normally arises as "How do we hear the word of God?" becomes for us the question, "What would we do if we heard it?"

Vagueness in this matter cannot be tolerated. There is too much *drift* in our lives. It may well be that, in some *vague* sense, we think we would do what God says were He to speak to us. But have we committed ourselves to a life of obedience? Have we accepted the extent to which the voice of God might disturb our plans? *Really?* Have we thought out what it would mean for all our family and social connections, and have we accepted *that?* It is only for such a one that guidance is fitting.

We borrow a few well-chosen words on this point from G. Campbell Morgan. Having mentioned that when God speaks to us His word comes as a disturbing element into our lives, he continues:

> You have never heard the voice of God, and you say: "The day of miracles is past. I am never disturbed. I make my own plans and live where I please and do as I like. What do you mean by a disturbing element?" . . . . Beloved, you are living still among the fleshpots and the garlic of Egypt. You are still in slavery . . . . You know no disturbing voice? God never points out for you a pathway altogether different from the one you had planned? Then, my brother, you are living still in the land of slavery, in the land of darkness.[4]

Perhaps we do not hear the voice because we don't *expect* to hear it. But perhaps we don't expect it because we know that we fully *intend* to run our lives on our own and never seriously considered anything else. The voice of God would therefore be an unwelcome intrusion into our plans. By contrast, we expect the great ones in The Way of Christ to hear that voice just because we see their lives wholly given up to doing what God wants.

Frank Laubach tells of the change which came over his life at the point when he resolved to do the will of God:

> As for me, I never lived, I was half dead, I was a rotting tree, until I reached the place where I wholly, with utter honesty, resolved and then re-resolved that I *would* find God's will, and I *would* do that will though every fibre in me said no, and I *would* win the battle in my thoughts. It was as though some deep artesian well had been struck in my soul . . . . You and I shall soon blow away from our bodies. Money, praise, poverty, opposition, these make no difference, for they will all alike be forgotten in a thousand years, but this spirit which comes to a mind set upon continuous surrender, this spirit is timeless.[5]

The Silence of Creation

But there still are those who understand the lowliness of God's greatness and the greatness of God's lowliness, and who besides this really do live to do the will of God; and yet they are troubled by the thought that God is afar off, that cold nature interposes itself as a barrier between us and Him. After the death of his dear friend A. H. Hallam, the poet Tennyson speaks as if he were addressed by the personage of Sorrow:

"The stars," she whispers, "blindly run";
A web is woven across the sky;
From out waste places comes a cry
And murmurs from a dying sun.

Especially in times when the word of God does not come and we are not at peace with Him, the very face of nature becomes cold and hard and forbidding: "And I will break the pride of your power; and I will make your heaven as iron, and your earth as brass: and your strength shall be spent in vain: for your land shall not yield her increase, neither shall the trees of the land yield their fruits" (Lev. 26:19-20). "And thy heaven that is over thy head shall be brass, and the earth that is under thee shall be iron. The Lord shall make the rain of thy land powder and dust: from heaven shall it come down upon thee, until thou be destroyed" (Deut. 28:23-24).

Then we cry out, "Oh that thou wouldest rend the heavens, that thou wouldest come down" (Isa. 64:1), but the heavens remain intact and God keeps His distance and nature rolls on. Amidst the ravages of war, accident, and physical and mental illness we suffer, shed our tears, and bury our loved ones and our hopes, while it seems that God is known only by His absence—anything but, we think, "our refuge and strength, a very present help in trouble" (Ps. 46:1).

The Warfare Between Science and Theology

But even beyond such an experience of the seemingly "godless" course of nature as this—common through all of the generations of humanity—there is a special burden of unbelief now born by Western civilization for several hundred years. This is the idea that it is *unscientific* to believe that God could speak to us or guide us: that scientific knowledge excludes the presence of God in the material universe of which we human beings are a pitifully small and insignificant part. The discovery of the immensity of space and of the forces of nature which appear to determine everything that happens and run their course with no assistance from the hand of a personal God can be quite overwhelming.

When the great French mathematician and astronomer, Laplace, presented the Emperor Napoleon with a copy of his work on celestial mechanics, the Emperor asked him where God fitted into his system. Laplace indignantly drew himself up and replied: "Sir, I have no need of any such an hypothesis!" And on the current model of the natural sciences they proceed without invoking God. You will not find any laboratory manual, any statistical analysis of social processes—even in a Christian school or seminary!—which introduces God *as a factor* in its calculations.

We may seem to have *imposed upon* us a picture of reality according to which humanity is encapsulated *within* a material world. God, on the other hand, is wholly *beyond* that material world which, for its part, runs by its own inherent mechanisms. We diagram this picture of reality as in figure 1.

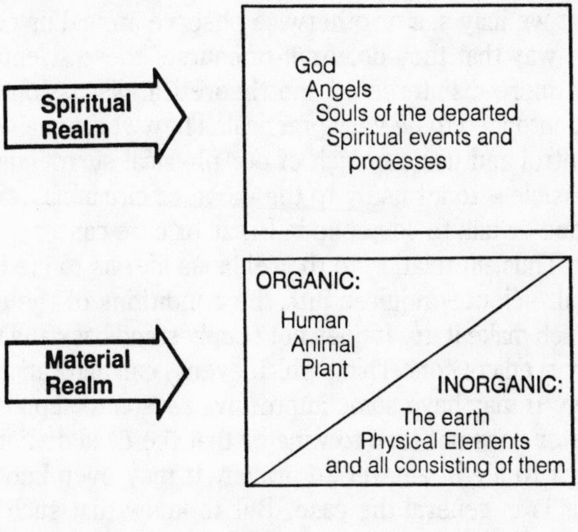

Figure 1

By eliminating the top half of this diagram we arrive at the world view of *naturalism,* which is generally assumed as a simple fact by contemporary secular humanists.

It is this view of a self-contained and compacted material universe, enclosing mankind within itself and under its total control that has been largely responsible for "the warfare between science and theology" during the last few centuries of Western history. In fact, there is nothing particularly scientific at all about the naturalistic view of reality. Just as in the study of chemistry we do not find God entered into the equation for a chemical process, so also we find no proof, or even a mention, of such a totally secular view of reality in any of our scientific textbooks. It is not the business of any science either to make such *total* claims about reality or to endeavor to prove them. This is generally recognized among scientists.

The natural sciences (and we can include the social sciences among them) have the task of developing laws of explanation, prediction, and control of the physical domain, including the social world. They want to give us an understanding of the reasons why the obvious events that we may see or otherwise observe around us occur in the way that they do. And, of course, these sciences are not mere disinterested and theoretical discussions; they are intended to be very practical. They would enable us to control and use as much of our physical surroundings as possible—to let us fly to the moon or circumnavigate the globe or talk to someone in Brazil or cure cancer.

Thus, in relation to the religious life, as to life in general, science inquires into the conditions of the events which make it up. It does not simply stand back and utter a priori edicts concerning which events can and cannot happen. It may have some impressive reason to suppose that water does not turn to wine or that the dead do not come back to life in answer to prayer. It may even know why this is in general the case. But to know that such things *cannot* happen suggests a total grasp of reality of *all* conditions for such events as are in question. And a total grasp of reality is—as a matter of simple fact—never assumed or proven in any science or group of sciences. Anyone who says it is, should be prepared to point to the science or sciences which do so and not stop with vague references to the "scientific view of the world."

The task of the Bible, by contrast, is to provide a consistent, specific, enduring, and impersonal witness in human language to the truth about God in His dealings with mankind: an infallible guide to men and women who wish to find Him and live in His ways. Science truly conflicts with the Bible if and insofar as it denies any truth essential to the biblical view of the divine-human relationship. This certainly includes God's creation of the world and of man, God's miraculous intervention in human history, the incarnation and resurrection of His uniquely begotten Son, His inspiration of and continuing care over the Scriptures and the Church, as well as the freedom of the human soul, life everlasting and God's availability to answer prayer and personally communicate with His earthly children.

The point to be clear on is that—contrary to what is often said—no *established scientific* truths rule out the basic, essential claims of the Bible about God and His relationship to mankind.

Of course it would take immense labors to bring the Bible and the science of any given time into a thorough and coherent relationship, and there are many ways in which misunderstandings can arise. There is, for example, the common misunderstanding of evolution as a theory of radical or ultimate *origins*. This misunderstanding is very common with people who have a preexisting bias against the Bible as a source of truth and who like to think of themselves as being scientific. But such persons are either ignorant or confused. For evolution *cannot* account for the origination of *every*thing, since it presupposes *some*thing already being there to evolve into something else, along with preexisting conditions within which the evolution might unfold. Evolution can occur only within a framework of things which already exist. Hence, a theory of evolution is not even a response to the same general question "What is the origin of the universe?" as is creation. The great Baptist theologian, A.H. Strong, long ago pointed out that "evolution is not a cause, but a method."[6]

Confusion and ignorance, whether among the faithful or their adversaries, must be dealt with *as* confusion and ignorance. There is nothing to be gained by trying to *reason* with them, whether for or against.

Confusion and ignorance aside, however, and returning to our main topic in this section, there was a period in recent intellectual history when physical reality *seemed* to many who were engaged in the study of it to be a wholly mechanical realm interposed between man and God—if there were a God. Given such a view of things, one of the greatest and most difficult issues we face in trying to think about guidance is *How does God "get through" to us?*

If *you* want to talk to someone in Germany, you will have to produce a chain of events in the physical substance, the inorganic matter, between here and there. You will perhaps begin by dialing a number on your telephone. This will cause electrical impulses to propagate themselves by various means across the intervening space. A physical apparatus located there will be sensitive to those impulses and will convert them into a form which your friend in Germany can hear or see and understand. The point is, to communicate—at least as is normally done—we must go through the intervening physical reality.

Even if I would speak directly to you, I must do the same. I make some sort of noise which strikes your eardrum. Somehow it causes you to think of specific things or events. I *cause* you to think, and that is what my communication with you consists of. What I have been doing in these pages is guiding you, guiding your thoughts. You have of course accepted my guidance and cooperated with me to some extent.

In our experience of art, the physical medium of communication—whether it is words written or spoken, color or form—becomes the field of creativity. When you go to a movie they darken the room, and you fix your eyes on the screen with its moving images. What are you then doing? You are accepting guidance through a physical medium. The variegated light reflecting from the screen into your eyes controls the processes of your experience.

The question we must face is, Is *that* the only way in which God can communicate with us? Does God always have to go through physical substance? Does the entire realm of organic and inorganic matter stand *between* us and God? *Where* is God in relation to that realm? How does God come into relation to us if He is far off from us? These are the most difficult questions which we take up in this chapter, but I hasten to say that I do *not* believe God *has to* go through physical intermediaries of any sort to reach us—though He obviously does do so on some occasions. The material world in which we are placed by Him permits Him to be "nearer" to us than even our own eyes, ears, and brain. It is "in him" that we "live, and move, and have our being" (Acts 17:28).

Our faith may all too easily fall victim to the tendency of the human mind to *spatialize* everything. If we think of God as being literally "outside" of the physical realm, then it will seem as if He were utterly out of reach for us and we out of reach for Him. The edge of the known universe is now thought to be something like thirteen or fourteen million light-years away. Beyond that, even light waves, traveling at the speed of 186,284 miles per second, never get to us. How then can we reach God or He us, if He is "out there"? The great scientist and Christian, Blaise Pascal, remarks:

> When I see the blind and wretched state of man, when I survey the whole universe in its

> dumbness and man left to its dumbness and man left to himself with no light, as though lost in this corner of the universe, without knowing who put him there, what he has come to do, what will become of him when he dies, incapable of knowing anything, I am moved to terror, like a man transported in his sleep to some terrifying desert island, who wakes up quite lost and with no means of escape. Then I marvel that so wretched a state does not drive people to despair.
>
> I see other people around me, made like myself. I ask them if they are any better informed than I, and they say they are not. Then these lost and wretched creatures look around and find some attractive objects to which they become addicted and attached. For my part I have never been able to form such attachments, and considering how very likely it is that there exists something besides what I can see, I have tried to find out whether God has left any traces of himself.[7]

The "traces" of God which have always stood forth to the earnest seeker consist in the purposeful order which appears within nature and history, as well as purposeful interventions which seem to show up in our individual lives. The *order* of events large and small throughout our world strongly suggests to those who are prepared to believe it that there is a providential and personal oversight of our world and our lives.

This is what the Apostle Paul has in mind when he says in his sermon on Mar's Hill in Athens that God has so arranged our world that we should seek the Lord and—as the *Jerusalem Bible* translates it—"by feeling [our] way towards him, succeed in finding him. Yet in fact he is not far from any of us, since it is in him that we live, and move, and exist" (Acts 17:27-28).

The New Testament presents Christ the Son as continuously "sustaining all things by his powerful word" (Heb. 1:3), and as the very "glue" of the universe, "In Him all things hold together" (sunistēmi, Col. 1:17). To utilize once again the wording of A.H. Strong:

> Christ is the originator and the upholder of the universe . . . . In him, the power of God, the universe became an actual, real thing, perceptible to others; and in him it consists, or holds together, from hour to hour. The steady will of Christ constitutes the law of the universe and makes it a cosmos instead of a chaos, just as his will brought it into being in the beginning.[8]

Communicating with God in an "Age of Science"

And now we come to the most important point for our present concerns. The current state of the physical sciences, in opposition to the crudely mechanical view which was dominant for several centuries past, is very congenial to the view of God's presence in His world that we find in the New Testament. Sir James Jeans interpreted the result of developments in physics during this present century as follows:

> Today there is a wide measure of agreement, which on the side of Physics approaches almost to unanimity, that the stream of knowledge is heading towards a non-mechanical reality; the universe begins to look more like a great thought than like a great machine. Mind no longer appears as an accidental intruder into the realm of matter; we are beginning to suspect that we ought rather to hail it as the creator and governor of the realm of matter.[9]

More recently, in his essay on "Remarks on the Mind-Body Question," Nobel Prize laureate Eugene Wigner points to a general recognition among physicists that thought or the mind is primary to physical reality: "It is not possible to formulate the laws of quantum mechanics in a fully consistent way without reference to consciousness." Princeton physicist John A. Wheeler even goes so far as to hold that subjective and objective reality, consciousness and matter, mutually create each other. Another physicist, Jack Sarfatti, remarks than "an idea of the utmost significance for the development of psycho-energetic systems . . . is that the structure of matter may not be independent of consciousness."[10]

Now we do not wish to make more of these recent interpretations of physics than is strictly warranted. In particular, there is here no suggestion that "physics proves" any theological position, or even that it *proves* matter to be dependent on mind, as the New Testament teaches. Our sole point is that *on contemporary views* of physical reality there is, so to speak, an "inside" or, better, a non-side to matter which allows for a *non-spatial and yet causal dimension* of the physical world—one which could well accommodate the biblical view of God's relation to His world in creation and sustenance. This lends some further support to our contention that there is no reason drawn from established truths of science to suppose that God *cannot* reach us to guide us and communicate with us. There is plenty of room left for God in the picture of the world presented to us by contemporary science. We live in the kind of material universe in which divine guidance is possible and, we would suggest, even reasonable to expect.

Now we must not suppose that such discussions as we have just gone through are irrelevant to our faith. A popular song says: "If you believe in things you don't understand you will suffer!" Perhaps this is an oversimplification, but the heart *is* connected with the head. A lack of understanding does weaken faith. Even though not everything can be understood, our faith will be strengthened by such understanding as it is possible to acquire. Science, vaguely understood, is a power of our age, a weighty authority—whether we like it or not. And if you really do believe that guidance is unscientific in the world in which you live, you are going to have great difficulty in making enough sense of it to deal with it in practice. It will be largely inasmuch as you come to understand that the whole of reality is something penetrated through and through by God that you can begin to open yourself up to the possibility of divine guidance.

We live in this world too much obsessed by practical concerns, governed by a fallen ideology—in part an ideology of the "scientific"—that shapes our minds away from God. We need done for our understanding what Elisha did for his young assistant on an occasion when they were in great danger. Speaking of guidance! The king of Syria was at war with Israel, but every time he laid his battle plans, Elisha would tell them to the king of Israel. The king of Syria naturally supposed that there was an Israelite spy in his confidence, but his aides all denied it, explaining that "Elisha, the prophet who is in Israel, tells the king of Israel the words that you speak in your bedroom" (2 Kings 6:12, *NASB*). This sort of thing is a part of the very life of the Bible, and if we cannot make sense of it in terms of what the experience of it would be like for us, then we will not be able to believe it—*really* believe it. Our very reading of the Bible may force us into skepticism about what is most important—a genuine relationship with God.

The king of Syria, for his part, went right to the heart of the problem: "Get Elisha!" So, when Elisha and his young helper stepped out the door one morning they were completely surrounded by Syrian troops. The Scripture account of what then happened is too good to do anything but quote: "When the attendant of the man of God had risen early and gone out, behold, an army with horses and chariots was circling the city. And his servant said to him, 'Alas, my master! What shall we do?' So he answered, 'Do not fear, for those who are with us are more than those who are with them.' Then Elisha prayed and said, 'O Lord, I pray, open his eyes that he may see.' And the Lord opened the servant's eyes, and he saw; and behold, the mountain was full of horses and chariots of fire all around Elisha" (2 Kings 6:15-17, *NASB*).

What did the young man see? I suggest that he was enabled to see the forces of God totally interpenetrating all of reality around him (even the Syrian army itself), whose every working was a movement within the encompassing Logos of God. How we need our Elishas today who, by life and teaching as well as prayer, might open our eyes to see the reality of God's presence all around us, in every bit of matter as well as beyond! We are like Jacob, wearily asleep on a rock in a desert ravine. He went to sleep in his sorrow, alienation, and loneliness, seeing only the physical landscape. In his dream—or was he only then *truly* awake?—he beheld the commerce of God with that ditch, and awakening cried out: "Surely the Lord is in this place, and I did not know it . . . . How awesome is this place! This is none other than the house of God, and this is the gate of heaven" (Gen. 28:16-17, *NASB*).

The angels keep their ancient places,
Turn a stone and start a wing,
'Tis ye, 'tis your estranged faces,
That miss the many splendored thing.[11]

Chaos in the Church

"Would God that all the Lord's people were prophets, and that the Lord would put his spirit upon them" (Num. 11:29).

One serious objection to the individual believer's living in a conversational relationship with God comes from a feeling that *this would lead to chaos in the church,* the community of believers. In 1 Peter the faithful are described as "living stones" (2:5, *RSV*). Think of trying to build a wall with stones or bricks which have a mind of their own. You fit them in here, and soon you find that they have waddled over there. Stones joined together in the wall find that they do not get along, and those set apart want to be together. The wall will fall.

Many a beleaguered pastor can understand what this all means. Perhaps the last thing he wants is for these "living stones" to be able to contradict him and criticize him on the basis of *their* "conversations with God." He will feel the weight of a logic which objects to the very essence of the Protestant (as in "protest") movement—a movement which continues apace today in an ever-increasing number of sects emerging within and upon the fringes of Christendom. This logic, driving toward a rigorous heirarchy of authority and subordination, naturally eventuates in one person alone who speaks for God and thus enforces conformity. What is in question here is nothing less than the model of leadership and authority that is to be adequate to the redeemed community living out the good news of God's reign in human life.

"Living stones" in conversation with God Himself begin to look much better—with all their problems—once we compare them to the alternatives, where the stones are dead. Dead stones are fine for the building of walls, but when we transfer over to the building of a community of persons, of a living temple for a living God, dead stones must be robots who simply do what they are told. This just will not do as a picture of the fellowship of Jesus Christ—a fellowship of friends united by knowledge and love, in free-hearted devotion to Christ.

Sheep Dogs or Shepherds?

Yet far too much in our examples and in our training for Christian leadership is oriented toward getting others merely to do as they are told. In this the Church far too greatly conforms to the leadership structures of the world. Indeed, *leader*ship is normally an empty euphemism as applied to our usual communal efforts, whether in a church or without. To manipulate and drive or manage people, is not the same thing as to *lead* them. The sheep dog nips and harasses the sheep, while the shepherd simply calls as he calmly walks ahead of the sheep. This distinction between the sheep dog and the shepherd is profoundly significant for how we think of our work as leaders of Christ's people. We must frequently ask ourselves which role we are fulfilling, and constantly return ourselves, if necessary, to the true posture of the shepherd.

When we lead in the style of the shepherd, our confidence is in one and only one thing: the word of the Great Shepherd coming through us to His sheep. We know that they know His voice, and will not follow another (John 10:1-14). We do not *want* them to follow another, even if that "other" is *us*. This supreme confidence, and this alone, frees us to be the ministers of Christ. We know that "every plant, which my heavenly Father hath not planted, shall be rooted up" (Matt. 15:13), and we have heard the Master say: "All that the Father giveth me shall come to me; and him that cometh to me I will in no wise cast out" (John 6:37). Thus we would never stoop to drive, manipulate, or manage, relying only upon the powers inherent in unassisted human nature (see 1 Pet. 4:11). The one who follows Christ in his or her ministry will substitute no Ishmaels for the promised Isaac. His authority over the flock is beyond successful challenge for God's purposes so long as he counts on God to do the work.

Not only so, but the undershepherd counts upon his flock to minister the word of God, along with "all good things" (Gal. 6:6), *to him*. Ministry of the word is never a one-way street when it is functioning rightly in a group. And it is at this point, of course, that we must leave the metaphor of sheep, lest they become sheep for slaughter. We are to lead "willingly," not for "filthy lucre," "neither as being lords over God's heritage, but being ensamples to the flock" (1 Pet. 5:2-3). In this way we are indeed to be "servant of all" (Mark 9:35).

How desperately out of line with these scriptural injunctions is so much current religious work. It must necessarily be so if those who lead do not utterly rely upon Christ's power and readiness to govern and guide His people effectively. They will invariably turn to controlling the flock through their own abilities to organize and drive—suitably clothed in a "spiritual" terminology and manner. And as is their faith, so shall it be. It will be in fact "my church" and "my ministry"—as is often explicitly said—and we will never know by experience how completely and in what manner *He* is lord of *His* church.

Leadership-Cultic or Christlike?

Spokesmen of the Christian community, as well as the general public, are frequently heard to lament the way in which "cults" turn their adherents into mindless robots. In our highly fragmented society, dominated by gadgetry and technology, lonely and alienated people are ready prey for any person who comes along and speaks with confidence about life and death—especially when they have some degree of glamour about them and profess to speak for God. There are now more than twenty-five hundred distinct cults active in the United States, all based upon the premise that God speaks to one or several central persons in a way not possible for the ordinary cult member. The ordinary member, on the other hand, is often taught not to trust his or her own mind or communications with God—unless within the context of the group with all its pressures toward conformity to the word from "on high." Frequently adherents are taught to accept the explicitly self-contradictory and what flies in the face of all common sense, if the leader says so.

Here we have a common factor between many of the cults and the yet more extreme groups which form around personalities such as Jim Jones and Charles Manson. But the more "mainline" religious groups, if they would be honest, should ask themselves to what extent their own models of leadership actually prepare the way for cult phenomena. I must ask myself, as a Christian minister, to what extent *I* might be prepared to have people put away their minds and their own individual experiences of guidance and communication with their Lord in order to secure a conformity and support adequate to maintain and enlarge *my* programs.

In contrast to the cultish mentality, consider the immense spiritual healthiness of that good man Charles Haddon Spurgeon:

> For my part I should loathe to be the pastor of a people who have nothing to say, or who, if they do say anything, might as well be quiet, for the pastor is Lord Paramount, and they are mere laymen and nobodies. I would sooner be the leader of six free men, whose enthusiastic love is my only power over them, than play the director to a score of enslaved nations.
>
> What position is nobler than that of a spiritual father who claims no authority and yet is universally esteemed, whose word is given only as tender advice, but is allowed to operate with the force of law? Consulting the wishes of others he finds that they are glad to defer to him. Lovingly firm and graciously gentle, he is the chief of all because he is the servant of all. Does not this need wisdom from above? What can require it more? David when established on the throne said, "[It is He] who subdueth my people under me," and so may every happy pastor say when he sees so many brethren of differing temperaments all happily willing to be under discipline, and to accept his leadership in the

> work of the Lord.
>
> . . . . Brethren, our system will not work without the Spirit of God, and I am glad it will not, for its stoppages and breakages call our attention to the fact of His absence. Our system was never intended to promote the glory of priests and pastors, but it is calculated to educate manly Christians, who will not take their faith at second-hand.[12]

What then are we to say? No doubt to have everyone conferring with God does risk disagreements and noncooperation. If the spirit of the prophets is subject to the prophets, the individual prophet may from time to time find himself earnestly questioned and examined—perhaps overturned—by those he is appointed to lead. It will then require a real security before man and authority from the Lord for him to lead, and a true humility—everyone thinking the other better than himself (Phil. 2:3)—in order for him to carry on with his work. But how came we to think that anything else than just this is the requirement for a minister of the Kingdom of God? For my part, I cannot help but say, This is exactly what we want of our leaders in the Church of the Lord Jesus Christ. It is exactly the spirit in which *He* led. The spirit and the manner of the Chief Shepherd *should* be the one adopted by the undershepherds. We can minister Christ only as we teach *what* He taught *in the manner* in which He taught it.

With this kind of spirit in the leaders, the individual members of the fellowship will have a correct and formative model of how *they* should respond to and bear their communications with God. Of course there is a subordination within the fellowship of believers. But it is not one which comes from a clever or crude struggle for ascendency. Rather, it stems solely from authority given by experience in The Way and by the speaking of God's word. If we but *count upon* the Christ whose Church is to bring that subordination to pass which is right, we shall then see actualized the true unity and power of the glorious Body of Christ, the living temple inhabited by God, which in its full realization is the end and aim of all human history.

It must never be forgotten that the social and outward dimension of the Church is not the whole—nor, finally, the basic dimension—of redemption. Ultimately, the social dimension, in all of its glory, is derived only from the individual's communion with God. The advice of Saint Francis de Sales to his disciple in The Way gives a proper practical balance. Describing as "inspirations" all of "those interior attractions, motions, reproaches and remorses, lights and conceptions which God excites in us," he directs her as follows:

> Resolve, then, Philothea, to accept with a ready heart all the inspirations it shall please God to send to you. When they come, receive them as ambassadors sent by the King of Heaven, who desires to enter into a marriage contract with you. Attend calmly to His proposals, think of the love with which you are inspired, and cherish the holy inspiration. Consent to the holy inspiration with an entire, a loving and a permanent consent.[13]

Then Saint Francis wisely proceeds to say, directing his friend back into the fellowship of the Church: "But before you consent to inspiration in things which are of great importance, or that are out of the ordinary way, always consult your advisor."[14] No man or woman is an island, but we are more than the sum of our relationships to others, even in the redemptive community. And our relationship to others—essential and helpful as they may be—finally rest upon our personal relationship to God Himself. When both relationships are right, we find perfect safety and

This full and perfect peace!
Oh, this transport all divine!
In a love that cannot cease,
I am His and He is mine.[15]

Questions

1. What are the limitations of guidance by means of "signs"?

2. What is meant by the "lowliness of God"?

3. What are two reasons it does not seem that God talks to some people?

4. "Evolution is not a theory of origins." Explain and discuss.

5. What is naturalism? Why is it hostile to biblical faith?

6. Some modern physicists believe that there is a real and definite aspect "to matter which allows for a non-spatial and yet causal dimension of the physical world." What issue is this statement addressing?

7. What are the problems in the church related to the "living stones" analogy?

8. What are the characteristics of cultic leadership? of Christlike leadership? Have you noticed any "cultic" tendencies in religious groups you are associated with?

9. God communicates within His cosmos. How? How does your concept of science influence the way in which you believe God relates to His creation?

Notes

1. Catherine Marshall, *A Man Called Peter* (New York: Fawcett Book Group, 1962), p. 24.
2. Agnes Sanford, *Sealed Orders* (Plainfield, NJ: Logos International, 1972), p. 98.
3. E. Stanley Jones, *A Song of Ascents* (Nashville, TN: Abingdon Press, 1968), p. 188.
4. G. Campbell Morgan, *How to Live* (Chicago: Moody Press, n.d.), p. 78.
5. Frank Laubach, *Letters By a Modern Mystic* (Syracuse, NY: New Reader's Press, 1955), p. 14.
6. A.H. Strong, *Christ in Creation* (Philadelphia: Griffith & Rowland Press, 1899), p. 163. On these matters see also Robert B. Fischer, *God Did It, But How?* (La Mirada, CA: Cal Media, 1981).
7. Blaise Pascal, *Pensees* (Baltimore, MD: Penguin Books, 1966), p. 88.
8. Strong, *Christ in Creation,* p. 3.
9. James Jean, *The Mysterious Universe* (New York: E.P. Dutton, 1932), p. 27.
10. Michael Talbot, *Mysticism and the New Physics* (New York: Bantam Books, 1981), from the introduction and chapter 1.
11. Francis Thompson, "The Kingdom of Heaven."
12. David Otis Fuller, ed., *Spurgeon's Lectures to His Students* (Grand Rapids, MI: Zondervan Publishing House, 1945), p. 187.
13. *Introduction to the Devout Life,* Ryan Translation (Garden City, NJ: Doubleday & Co., 1957), p. 106.
14. Ibid.
15. G. Wade Robinson, "Loved with Everlasting Love."

CHAPTER 5

THE STILL SMALL VOICE AND ITS RIVALS

Therefore Eli said unto Samuel, Go, lie down: and it shall be, if he call thee, that thou shalt say, Speak, Lord, for thy servant heareth (1 Samuel 3:9).

And, behold, the Lord passed by, and a great and strong wind rent the mountains, and brake in pieces the rocks before the Lord; but the Lord was not in the wind: and after the wind an earthquake; but the Lord was not in the earthquake: and after the earthquake a fire; but the Lord was not in the fire: and after the fire a still small voice. And it was so, when Elijah heard it, that he wrapped his face in his mantle, and went out, and stood in the entering in of the cave. And, behold, there came a voice unto him, and said, What doest thou here, Elijah? (1 Kings 19:11-13).

Guidance Is a Process

We have seen that guidance is a process where some person or thing or sequence of events is brought to follow a definite course. In this inclusive sense, the train is guided by the rails upon which it runs, the driver guides the automobile, the writer guides the pen or typewriter, the radar guides the airplane, the stars guide the ship, the teacher guides the class and the parent guides the child. God *can,* certainly, *determine* the course of our lives by manipulation of our thoughts and feelings or by arranging external circumstances, what is often called the "closing" and "opening" of doors in the "sovereign will" of God. But He *can* and *does* also guide us not by a blind determination alone but by *addressing* us.

But God addresses individual human beings by various ways: in dreams, visions, voices, through the Bible, extraordinary events, and so forth. This is a plain fact about mankind's general experience of God, and also is clearly marked out in the biblical accounts. Confusion about the *significance* of the various ways in which God encounters us, communicates with us, causes many problems for serious seekers of His guidance.

In a letter sent out by the staff of *Guideposts* magazine we are told of an ordinary suburban housewife who one day for reasons unknown to her, began to weep and continued weeping for four days. As the letter relates it:

> On the morning of the fourth day, alone in her living room, there was a sudden hum and crackle in the air. She saw a ball of white light through a window, spraying showers of multicolored light in its wake and approaching her with amazing speed. Then it was right there, beside her, and as she looked at it she saw a face.
>
> "He is perfect," was her first thought. His forehead was high. His eyes were large but she

> could not fix their color any more than she could the color of the sea. His features were lost in the overwhelming impression of life brimming over with power and freedom.
>
> Instantly she knew this was Jesus. She saw His utter lack of condemnation; saw that nothing she had ever done or ever would do could alter the absolute caring or the unconditional love in His eyes.

According to the account, Jesus was present with her in the manner described for three months, and then His presence began to fade. When this lady, named Virginia Lively, last saw Him, He said to her, "I will always be with you." She, Thaddeus-like (John 14:22), asked how she would know it if she could no longer see him. He replied, "You will see me," and He was gone.

Some years later, while speaking to a church group, she found His eyes looking into hers again; but the eyes belonged to a woman in the second row. "And suddenly she saw His eyes looking at her from the eyes of every person in the room."[1]

Now it is very interesting and useful, for our study, to observe the varying reactions which a story such as this occasions. Some immediately conclude that the whole thing is of the devil because "Satan himself is transformed into an angel of light" (2 Cor. 11:14). These overlook the fact that light only serves as Satan's disguise because God *is* light (1 John 1:5), and because we are children of light (Eph. 5:8), saints in light (Col. 1:12), and His messengers are a flame of fire (Ps. 104:4).

Others will suppose that Mrs. Lively just hallucinated or suffered a "nervous breakdown" due to stress she could not cope with or even face. Some will simply be at a loss as to *what* was going on with her, but remain unconvinced that Jesus Christ Himself came to her on the occasions described.

At the other end of the spectrum there are those who will consider her as especially favored by God above all who have not had such an experience. They may go so far so to confuse the medium with the message and worship the experience rather than Him who was allegedly present through it. These people often feel spiritually inferior until something similar happens to them. They will be tempted to try to *make* it happen, and perhaps will even deceive themselves into *faking* it. They may judge those without such an experience to be incapable of any significant spiritual ministry or service to God, or of going to heaven when they die. Experiences of this unusual type obviously pose problems for the understanding of guidance, as for the understanding of the spiritual life generally.

Now we are far from wishing to deny that such "spectacular" experiences occur and are, sometimes, given by God. But it is a major point of this book that the "still small voice"—or the "interior" voice, as it also is sometimes called—is the primary form (preferred by God), in which God individually addresses those who walk with Him in a mature, conversational relationship, proclaiming and showing forth the reality of the Kingdom of God. We must therefore carefully consider it in relation to the other ways—its "rivals"—in which God personally encounters man.

We hasten to add that the "voice" need not be a very self-conscious matter, and one need have no theory or doctrine *about* it in order for it to occur. When it came to little Samuel he did not know what it was or even that there was any such a thing. And indeed, I believe it possible for one who regularly interacts with the voice of God to not even recognize it as something "special." In contrast to those who have the more spectacular experiences, one often finds a reluctance to speak much about the inner voice in those most adept at the divine/human conversation. And this is completely as it should be. God's guidance is not for "show and tell," any more than are intimate interchanges between persons generally.

But where, as here, an understanding of guidance is sought, discussion of the voice is indispensable. Our procedure will be to consider the various ways in which God addresses men and women, in the course of guiding them, in the hope of gaining a better general understanding of the nature and function of *the* one way which is most suited and preferred for communion between God and man. We will begin by providing a brief—and undoubtedly an imprecise and incomplete—catalogue of epiphanies, taken chiefly from the Bible.

However, before beginning this discussion we must remind ourselves to read the biblical accounts which we are about to consider as if what is described were happening to *us*. We must make the conscious effort to think that such things might happen to us, and to imagine what it would be like if they did. And this is at first difficult, for we are accustomed to thinking that God does those marvelous things only with *other* people. So we must give ourselves a little talking to, pointing out that Elijah, Moses, and Paul were, as we have noted, in themselves people "subject to like passions as we are." When misunderstood or mistreated they felt as we do. They too experienced hunger, weariness, nervousness, confusion, and fear. They too doubted their abilities and their self-worth. They too—witness Moses and Gideon—often said, "Oh, no! Not *me*. I can't do it."

Occasionally a Saul gets knocked off his horse; but as a general rule God is not going to run over us. And if we are not open to the possibility of God's addressing us in whatever way *He* chooses, then we may walk right by the burning bush instead of, like Moses, saying, "I will now turn aside, and see this great sight, why the bush is not burnt" (Exod. 3:3). We may take the voice of God to be someone's radio turned up too loud, or to be some accidental noise. It is when we *seek* God, and thus are prepared to go out of our way in examining those things which might be His overtures toward us, that He promises to be found; and we can only seek Him if we believe that He might explicitly address *us* in ways suitable to His purposes in our lives.

With this reminder, and a plea for the use of our imagination to identify with the experiences of persons whom we shall be considering, we turn now to six ways in which people are addressed by God within the biblical record. These are:

1. Phenomenon plus voice
2. Supernatural messenger or angel
3. Dreams and visions
4. Audible voice
5. The human voice
6. The "spirit of man."

Phenomenon Plus Voice

This category of divine/human encounter is, of course, richly represented in the events of Scripture. The Abrahamic covenant was solemnized upon such an occasion: a fire from God consumed the sacrifice Abraham had prepared while God stated the promise to Abraham and his seed (Gen. 15:12-21). Moses received his call to deliver Israel by the hand of God from Egypt before the burning bush from which God spoke (Exod. 3:3-6). The nation of Israel as a whole heard God's voice from within a mountain on fire (Deut. 5:23). Ezekiel was spoken to in the context of a meteorological display that defies all but poetic description (Ezek. 1–2). At the baptism of Jesus the heavens appeared to open up, and the Spirit visibly descended upon Him in conjunction with "a voice" from heaven that said: "This is my beloved Son, in whom I am well pleased" (Matt. 3:17). Saul's encounter with Christ on the road to Damascus involved a blinding light from heaven and an audible voice heard not only by Saul but by those with him as well (Acts 9:3-8).

Supernatural Messenger or Angel

In his recent book on angels Mortimer J. Adler describes the opposition from his distinguished scholarly colleagues when, for a major publication, he wished to include angels among the great ideas of Western man.[2] There is no doubt whatsoever that, purely in terms of the amount of attention which they have received—not only in religion, but also in art, literature, and philosophy—angels deserve the place in Western civilization assigned to them by Adler. And it certainly is not going too far to describe the Bible itself as a book full of angels.

Strictly speaking, *angel* means only "emissary" or "messenger," but it is normally understood that these messengers, while persons, are not mere human beings. They are supernatural beings, and God addresses man through them.

Sometimes, in the biblical record, it is difficult to decide whether an angel or the Lord Himself is on the scene. Thus, for example, we have Genesis 18 where three "men" suddenly appear at the door of Abraham's tent. In the middle of this chapter the text casually shifts from "they" and "the men" to "the Lord." And there then follows the well-known dialogue between Abraham and the Lord concerning the fate of Sodom. Strangely, at the opening of chapter 19 it is only two "angels"—two who apparently were with "the Lord"—that show up to Lot in Sodom to finish off the episode. Hebrews 13:2 is usually taken as referring back to this passage in Genesis when it exhorts us to "be not forgetful to entertain strangers: for thereby some have entertained angels unawares."

Joshua, before the city of Jericho (Josh. 5:13-15), encounters "a man . . . with his sword drawn in his hand," who has come to help as "captain of the host of the Lord," and who directs Joshua to take off his shoes because of the holiness of the ground where he is standing. The "host of the Lord" consisted, presumably, of angels—no doubt the same as those legions which stood at the beck and call of our incarnate Lord (Matt. 26:53). A few verses later (Josh. 6:2), this "captain" now seems to be "the Lord" Himself, giving that famous and unorthodox military strategy whereby the walls of Jericho were to be brought down.

Man is so commonly addressed by angels in Scripture that here we shall list only a few more of the outstanding cases: Balaam (Num. 22:22-35); Gideon (Judg. 6:11-24); the parents of Samson (Judg. 13); Isaiah (Isa. 6:6-13); Daniel (Dan. 9:20-27); Joseph (Matt. 1:20-25); Zacharias (Luke 1:11-20); Mary (Luke 1:26-38); the women at the empty tomb (Matt. 28:2-5); Peter (Acts 5:19-20); and Paul (Acts 23:11; 27:23-24).

It is important to observe that encounters with angels seem to occur in an otherwise "normal" state of mind, as distinct from dreams and visions—although the content of the conversations recorded sometimes suggests (as with Gideon, with Samson's parents, and with Zacharias) that the people involved felt things to be getting a bit out of control.

Dreams and Visions

These two categories of divine communications can perhaps be treated together, since our purposes do not lead us into any scholarly depth or precision. Sometimes they seem to coincide, perhaps because they often come at night and the recipients may have been unable to tell with certainty whether they were awake or asleep. Thus Paul: "And a vision appeared to Paul in the night; There stood a man of Macedonia, and prayed him, saying, Come over into Macedonia, and help us" (Acts 16:9; see also Acts 18:9; 2 Cor. 12:1). Both visions and dreams involve a trancelike condition which stands off clearly from ordinary waking consciousness.

On the other hand, some visions clearly are not dreams, as with Ananias, to whom the Lord spoke in a vision (Acts 9:10-13), and Peter in his rooftop "trance"

(Acts 10:9-18), also specifically called a vision (v. 19). And many dreams are not visions, as was the case with Jacob's dream (Gen. 28), Joseph's dreams (Gen. 37), those of his jailmates (Gen. 40), Pharaoh's (Gen. 41), and Nebuchadnezzar's (Dan. 4).

Gustave Oehler points out that the difference between a dream and a vision is not sharply marked out in the Bible.[3] However, as he concedes, the dream is regarded as a lower form of communication from God than a vision. Both are abnormal states of consciousness, but the dream characteristically requires greater interpretation, often of great difficulty in a manner which the vision does not.

By the time of Jeremiah, the understanding of the ways in which God speaks to us had progressed to the point where the "dreaming" prophet was treated with some contempt. The dream is like straw or chaff when compared to the "wheat" of God's *word* (Jer. 23:25-32). The word, on the other hand, is like fire, like a hammer that crushes the rock. The dream has no comparable power. Oehler sees emerging here "the principle that a clear consciousness when receiving revelation is placed higher than ecstasy or other abnormal states of mind."[4] This is a point that is very important to keep in mind in our efforts to understand our own experiences of God's communications and the significance of the different ways in which He meets us.

Audible Voice

However we are to understand the mechanisms involved, it is clear that upon occasion God has addressed man through what was experienced as an audible voice alone. Something like this, though involving an angel "in heaven," seems to have occurred with Abraham on Mount Moriah, about to sacrifice Isaac his son (Gen. 22:11,15).

A most touching, instructive, and profound story is that of the child Samuel learning to recognize God's voice which he clearly experienced as an audible voice (1 Sam.

3). As this young boy lay on his pallet "ere the lamp of God went out in the temple of the Lord, where the ark of God was" (v. 3), he heard his name called out. He rose and ran to his old master, Eli, thinking that it was he who had called. This was during a period in the history of Israel when God rarely spoke, and no visions were occurring. Such things as voices and visions were not commonly discussed. Hence, "Samuel did not yet know the Lord, neither was the word of the Lord yet revealed unto him" (v. 7).

On the third time that Samuel came to Eli, assuring him that he *had* certainly called him, Eli recognized what was happening. "Therefore Eli said unto Samuel, Go, lie down: and it shall be, if he call thee, that thou shalt say, Speak, Lord; for thy servant heareth. So Samuel went and lay down in his place. And the Lord came, and stood, and called as at other times, Samuel, Samuel. Then Samuel answered, Speak; for thy servant heareth" (1 Sam. 3:9-10). With this, there began one of the most remarkable careers of any person who has ever lived before the Lord, justifying fully the use of the phrase "conversational relationship" between God and man.

The Human Voice

We have seen that an audible, nonhuman voice was present both at the baptism of Jesus and on the Damascus Road. But no means of communication between God and man is more commonly used in the Bible or the history of the Church than the human voice itself. In such cases God and man speak *conjointly.* The word is at once the word of God, God speaking, and the word of a man who is speaking. The two do not exclude each other any more than humanity and divinity exclude one another in the person of Jesus Christ. We can say that God speaks *through* man, as long as that is not understood to rule out man speaking with God, and possibly even—in some important sense—through God. The relationship must not be understood as essentially mechanical with God simply *using* man as we might use a telephone.

Samuel Shoemaker has written this excellent description of our experience of God in this connection:

> Something comes into our own energies and capacities and expands them. We are laid hold of by Something greater than ourselves. We can face things, create things, accomplish things, that in our own strength would have been impossible . . . . The Holy Spirit seems to mix and mingle His power with our own, so that what happens is both a heightening of our own powers, and a gift to us from outside. This is as real and definite as attaching an appliance to an electrical outlet, though of course such a mechanical analogy is not altogether satisfactory.[5]

Now we may say with assurance that this union with the human voice and human language is the primary *objective* way in which God addresses man. That is, of all the modes in which the message concerned comes from *outside* the mind or personality of the person addressed, in the most common of cases it comes through another human being; and this manner of its coming is best suited to the purposes of God precisely because it most engages the faculties of free, intelligent beings, socially interacting in the work of God as His co-laborers and friends. This is obvious from the contents of the Bible, and the Bible is itself a case of God speaking *with* man, many men, in its own composition.

In the encounter of Moses with God through the burning bush, his last line of protest against the assignment that God was giving to him was that he did not speak well: "Please, Lord, I have never been eloquent, neither recently nor in time past, nor since Thou has spoken to

Thy servant; for I am slow of speech and slow of tongue" (Exod. 4:10, *NASB*). The Lord's reply was that He, after all, made mouths, and presumably could have His way with them: "Now then go, and I, even I, will be with your mouth, and teach you what you are to say" (v. 12).

When Moses still begged God to send someone else, God angrily gave him Aaron as *his* spokesman: "You are to speak to him [Aaron] and put the words in his mouth; and I, even I, will be with your mouth and his mouth, and I will teach you what you are to do. Moreover, he shall speak for you to the people; and it shall come about that he shall be as a mouth for you, and you shall be as God to him. And you shall take in your hand this staff, with which you shall perform the signs" (15-17).

Some New Testament passages suggest that the Apostle Paul also was not an eloquent person. We know from his own statements that, whether by choice or necessity, he came among the Corinthians "not . . . with superiority of speech or of wisdom," but was with them "in weakness and in fear and in much trembling. And my message and my preaching were not in persuasive words of wisdom, but in demonstration of the Spirit and of power, that your faith should not rest on the wisdom of men, but on the power of God" (1 Cor. 2:1-5, *NASB*). His only confidence was in God speaking *with* him, in unison with him, when he spoke.

It is significant, I believe, that those chosen by our Lord to bear His message and carry on His work were "unlearned and ignorant men" (Acts 4:13). The pattern seems amply to prove that in selecting them God would have no mistake made about where they got their words and authority. He would use men, and dignify them by the association. But just as this is wholly suitable to His redemptive purposes, so it is wholly appropriate that everyone should be clear about the source of power involved.

There must be no misallocation of glory, for that would

destroy the *order* that is in beatitude in the life of blessing: "He that glorieth, let him glory in the Lord" (1 Cor. 1:31). The success of the redemptive plan therefore requires that possibly some, but "not *many* wise men after the flesh, not *many* mighty, not *many* noble are called" (1 Cor. 1:26) into the work. The two people most responsible for the human authorship of the Bible, Moses and Paul, were accordingly weak with words that they might have the best chance of clinging constantly to their support in God who spoke in union with them.

In some parts of the Bible record those who speak for God seem compelled by force, as we see in the case of Balaam. Balak, king of Moab, offered Balaam great riches and honor to curse Israel, for he knew that Balaam spoke in unison with God, so that "he whom thou blessest is blessed, and he whom thou cursest is cursed" (Num. 22:6). Balaam was obviously greatly tempted by the offer, for even after God told him *not* to go to Balak and *not* to curse Israel because Israel was blessed (22:12-14), he toyed with the idea; and he at least *thought* that he had God's permission to go to Balak (v. 20). But even while in Balak's camp he was *unable* to curse Israel. He explained to Balak that he did not have "any power at all to say anything. The word that God puts in my mouth, that shall I speak." And when after great preparation the moment came for him to curse Israel, only a stream of blessings came forth (Num. 23:7-10)—to the exasperation of Balak (vv. 11,25).

It would be a great mistake, however, to take these and similar cases to mean that the one who speaks with God, and thus speaks the word *of* God, literally cannot help speaking. Perhaps this is true in some cases, and it is true that he or she cannot force God to speak with them. But the compulsion upon them to speak, though often great, is normally still resistable. They are not mere *tools*.

The experience of Jeremiah in this connection has been replicated innumerable times in the experience of those who understand what it is to speak for and with God. Speaking God's word had made him a laughingstock and a subject of derision on the part of those who knew him. Hence, he resolved to speak no more for the Lord. "But if I say, 'I will not remember Him or speak any more in His name,' then in my heart it becomes like a burning fire shut up in my bones; and I am weary of holding it in, and I cannot endure it" (Jer. 20:9, *NASB*).

Thus the word of the Lord is often treated by the prophets as a *burden*. Later, in his sermon against the false prophets, Jeremiah cries: "My heart is broken within me, I tremble in all my bones I am like a drunken man, a man overcome with wine—because of Yahweh and his holy words" (Jer. 23:9, *JB*).

But, on the other hand, the prophet may also exalt in the power he feels surging within him, as did Micah: "I am filled with power—with the Spirit of the Lord—and with justice and courage to make known to Jacob his rebellious act, even to Israel his sin" (Mic. 3:8, *NASB*). Jeremiah also, we recall, had experienced the word to be of great power, like a fire that scorches, and like a hammer that breaks rocks.

In a later chapter we must explore in detail the idea of the word of God as an agency, a substantial power, in the cosmos and in human affairs: an agency which could "come unto John . . . in the wilderness" (Luke 3:2), have dominion over unclean spirits (Luke 4:33-36) like the finger of God (Luke 11:20), be spirit and be life (John 6:63,68), increase (Acts 6:7), grow and multiply (Acts 12:24), not be bound in prison (2 Tim. 2:9), function as the sword of the Spirit (Eph. 6:17)—being more dexterous and powerful than any mere two-edged human sword, since it has a life of its own and is so acute that it can dissect thoughts and intentions (Heb. 4:12)—and simultaneously hold all of creation together (Col. 1:17).

This picture of the word of God must be closely examined before we conclude our study. But for now we rest with the fact that that word can and does come to us through the living personality, mind, and body of other human beings as they in unison with God speak to us.

The Spirit of Man

The final instrumentality here considered through which God addresses us is our own spirits—our own thoughts and feelings, as well as toward events and persons around us. And this, I believe, is the primary *subjective* mode through which God addresses man. That is, of all the ways in which the message concerned comes from *within* the experience of the person addressed—such as dreams and visions or other mental states—it most commonly comes, in those who live in harmony with God, through their own *thoughts* and the attendant feelings. And of the subjective routes, this manner of coming is best suited to the redemptive purposes of God because it most engages the faculties of free, intelligent beings in the work of God as His co-laborers and friends.

The King James version of Proverbs 20:27 says: "The spirit of man is the candle of the Lord, searching all the inward parts of the belly." This is better put in the *Jerusalem Bible:* "Man's spirit is the Lamp of Yahweh, searching his deepest self." In a passage of great importance and depth, the Apostle Paul makes a comparison between man and God with respect to self-knowledge. "For who among men knows the thoughts of a man except the spirit of the man, which is in him? Even so the thoughts of God no one knows except the Spirit of God" (1 Cor. 2:11, *NASB*). But, in contrast to the proverb, where *the Lord's* use of *our* spirit is emphasized, Paul then points out that we have received the Spirit of God, and concludes that we can therefore search out and know the very mind of God. Quoting the question from Isaiah 40:13, "For who has known the mind of the Lord, that he should instruct Him?" the apostle replies: "But we have the mind of Christ" (1 Cor. 2:16, *NASB*).

Thus the Lord uses our self-knowledge to search us out and reveal to us the truth about ourselves and our world. And, on the other hand, *we* are able to use His knowledge of Himself—made available to us in Christ—to understand *His* thoughts and intentions toward us, and to help us see His workings in our world. In the union and communion of the believer with God, they are unified and reciprocally inhabit each other as Jesus prayed: "That they all may be one; as thou, Father, art in me, and I in thee, that they also may be one in us: that the world may believe that thou hast sent me" (John 17:21). His laws are increasingly, as we grow in grace, the constitution of our hearts, His love is our love, His faith our faith. Our very awarenesses of our actions and intentions and surroundings then bear within them the view which God takes, and brings things into the clarity of *His* vision as a candle illumines for us what is present upon our dinner table.

The spirit of man is the candle of the Lord in whose light we see ourselves and our world as God sees, and hence we are addressed *by Him,* spoken to by Him, through *our own* thoughts.

This you can test by experiment. Anyone who will begin to pray that God will illumine them as to the nature and meaning of the processes that go on in their own soul will begin to understand and see their spirit functioning as the candle of the Lord. Its self-awareness passes about in every part of the mind where it touches their family, where it touches their possessions, where it touches their profession, where it touches their health, their fear of death, where it touches their attitudes toward God, where it touches their sexual life, where it touches their reputation, and their concern about their appearance—all of these things and more.

Our spirit, as a candle in the Lord's hands, may turn to many other things than our own internal condition, although the primary point of the passage from Proverbs deals with the illumination of the inner life. Russ Johnston points out the importance of ***recurrent thoughts*** in God's guidance of His children:

> We would see wonderful results if we would just deal with the thoughts that continue in our minds in a godly manner. But most people don't . . . . As thoughts come into your mind and continue, ask God, "Do you really want me (or us) to do this?" Most of us just let those thoughts collapse—and God looks for someone else to stand in the gap.[6]

A well-intended but mistaken teaching about our thoughts has done much harm to the understanding of divine guidance. The great Puritan minister Thomas Goodwin wrote a discourse on *The Vanity of Thoughts,* taking as his text Jeremiah 4:14: "How long shall your vain thoughts lodge within you?"[7] Goodwin is fairly careful in the manner in which he describes these "vain" thoughts, but he leaves the impression, which is agreed to by many, that if a thought is *our* thought, it could not possibly be trusted. Does not Isaiah 55:8 tell us that "My [God's] thoughts are not your [man's] thoughts"? Does not Genesis 6:5 tell us of those that lived before the flood that "every imagination of the thoughts of [man's] heart was only evil continually"? And does not Jeremiah also tell us that our hearts are desperately wicked, beyond our powers of comprehension (17:9)?

There is an important point in all of this, emphasizing the difference between God's view of things and that of the normal fallen man *apart from* God. But this point must not be allowed to obscure the simple *fact* that God comes to us precisely in and through *our* thoughts, perceptions, and experiences, and ultimately can come to us only through them, for they are the substance of our lives. We are, therefore, to be transformed by the renewing of *our minds* (Rom. 12:2). His gracious incursions into our souls can make our thoughts His thoughts, and He can even help us learn to distinguish when the thought is *only* ours, and when it is also His. We shall later discuss at length how we can know which thoughts are from God; but when thoughts recur, we should always stop prayerfully to consider whether or not they may be an appearance of the Lord's candle, or whether they may have some other significance. Repetitious thoughts must not be disregarded.

The thoughts and attendant feelings of the spirit surrendered to God make it as if God were walking through the personality with a candle, directing our attention to one thing and then another. And as we become used to the idea that God is friendly and helpful, that He is there to straighten, to inform and correct, that God really does love us, then we can begin to pray as the psalmist did, "Search me, O God, and know my heart" (139:23). We are praying: "Bring the candle to bear upon this, please," somewhat as we might go to the dentist or physician and say, "Search me, please, and see if there are needed corrections of my physical condition. Find out what is needed and repair it." Here our own spirit works together with the Almighty God, utilizing our own thoughts and feelings to bring the truth of His word and understanding to bear upon our heart and life and world.

Having brought before us some major ways in which, in the biblical record, God addresses the conscious mind and will of man in order to inform him and guide him, let us now give some thought to their meaning for our quest for guidance.

God Speaks Today

The first thing which must be said is that *there is no foundation* in Scripture, in reason, or in the nature of things *why any or all of these types of experiences might not be used by God today* to communicate with His creatures and His children. No one should be alarmed or automatically thrown into doubt by such things coming to them, or by reports that other persons have experienced them. Here as always, with hearts at peace, we simply follow the Pauline admonition to "Prove all things; hold fast that which is good" (1 Thess. 5:21).

It is true that the existence and history of the Church and the presence of the full written Scripture changes the circumstances of and gives new dimensions to the way in which God deals with human beings. But there is nothing *in* Scripture which, by explicit statement or by implication, declares the biblical modes of God's guidance to man to be superseded and abolished by the presence of the Church and the close of the scriptural canon.

This is simply a fact, as it is simply a fact that God's children have continued to the present age to be addressed by God in all or several of the ways common to biblical characters. The testimony of these individuals—where they are generally admitted to be honest and clear-minded and devout, including many of the very greatest of Christians throughout the ages—should not be discarded in favor of a mere rigid dogma with no scriptural foundation, and which, moreover, substitutes for the gospel word of power the safety and deadness of the ponderous scholar and the letter-learned scribe.

The close of scriptural canon marks the point in the ongoing divine/human conversation where the *general* principles and doctrines that constitute the substance of faith and practice in the following of Christ are so adequately stated in human language that nothing more need be said *in general.* It is the faith of the biblical Christian that nothing further will be said by God to extend or contradict them. But the biblical Christian is not just one who holds certain beliefs *about* the Bible. Rather he or she is one who leads that kind of life shown forth in the Bible: one of personal, intelligent interaction with God. Anything less than this makes a mockery of the priesthood of the believer.

A book on *Decision Making and the Will of God*

describes a "traditional view" according to which:

> the Bible only reveals God's moral will, but His ideal will is more specific. And direct revelation (i.e., verbal communication by God to the individual) is not to be sought or expected. So when someone holding the traditional view says, "I have discovered God's will concerning which school I should attend," he is not claiming to have received supernatural revelation, nor did he find such leading from a direct statement of Scripture.[8]

The "traditional view" is presented by this author as if it held "inner impressions" to be the mode of direct revelation from God, even though the term "verbal communication" is used in the above quotation. He proceeds to say that "the problem with the traditional view is not that it recognizes the reality of inner impressions, but that it requires too much of them," namely, that they should provide "objective guidance pointing to one 'right' decision."[9]

Now the emphasis of this book is upon decision making. Speaking quite generally, however, it seems to me that one of the most damaging things we can do to the spiritual prospects of anyone is to suggest or teach that God will *not* deal with them specifically, personally, intelligibly, and consciously, or that they cannot *count on* Him to do so. Once we have conveyed this idea to them, it is absurd to go on to try to lead them into a personal relationship with God.

Conversing with God

Rosalind Rinker relates how after years of service on the mission field, and many fruitless efforts at a satisfactory prayer life, she found herself rebellious and spiritually empty. Then, through a serious illness and other grave difficulties, "God began to take care of my rebellions through His great love. *He began to teach me to listen to His voice.*"[10] Almost by "chance," as she was praying with a friend for some of their students, she interrupted the friend's prayer with thanksgiving on a point that was being prayed for. After a moment of awkward silence, and after they had sat back and laughed with great relief, they settled down again to prayer, but now "with a sense of joy, of lightness, of the Lord's presence very near." They asked in prayer if the Lord was trying to teach them something about prayer. "Should we give Thee more opportunity as we are praying to get Thy ideas through to us? Would that give the Holy Spirit more opportunity to guide us as we pray?" Then Miss Rinker stopped praying, and said to her friend:

> Do you know what? I believe the Lord taught us something just now! Instead of each of us making a prayer-speech to Him, let's talk things over with Him, including Him in it, as we do when we have a conversation.[11]

I can personally recall when her book *Prayer: Conversing with God* came upon the scene in the United States, and how group after group was brought to life as they learned to listen to God as well as "make prayer-speeches" at Him. Their talk of a personal relationship with God now had real, objectively shareable content.

Nowhere is it more important to be in a conversational relationship with God than in our prayer life. Often God does not give us what we ask for, but I believe that He will always answer, always *respond* to us. It is interesting that we commonly speak of *answered* prayer only where we are given our requests. Is there to be no response then when the request is denied? Some people are heard to say that God's *silence* is an answer in these cases. But I think that God will normally *tell us* something when He does not give us our requests, and we will hear it and grow through it *if* we have learned to know His voice. This was certainly true in the case of Paul's "thorn in the flesh," which he three times begged the Lord to remove from him (2 Cor. 12:7-8). The Lord was not silent to Paul: "*And he said unto me,* My grace is sufficient for thee: for my strength is made perfect in weakness" (v. 9, italics added).

God is not impassive toward us like the heathen idol, but calls us to grow into a life of personal interchange with Him that does justice to the idea of our being *His children.*

Is the Bible Enough?

One of the strange premises put forward to disallow any significant continuing usage of voices, visions, dreams, prophetic personages, and individual thoughts *as* communications from God is that these, allegedly, are no longer *needed.* "We have the Bible and we have the church. Let *them* speak for God." But a number of things should be said in response to this.

First of all, if by "needed" we refer to what is minimally required to enable human beings to know God, this, according to the Bible itself, is available independently of the Bible and of the Church. Hence they too would not be "needed," and yet here they are. As the *New English Bible* renders Romans 1:19-21: "For all that may be known of God by men lies plain before their eyes: indeed God himself has disclosed it to them. His invisible attributes, that is to say his everlasting power and deity, have been visible, ever since the world began, to the eye of reason, in the things he has made. There is therefore no possible defence for their conduct; knowing God, they have refused to honour him as God, or to render him thanks."

But if by "needed" we refer to what is required to constitute a truly personal redemptive relationship between God and the individual soul, then certainly the existence of the Bible and the Church is *not* enough. These must at least, in addition to merely *being there,* have an individualized function in the life of each believer. And in order for this to happen they must become the instrumentality through which God personally and uniquely addresses each individual.

Referring to the question, "Were not the miracles and gifts of the Spirit only for the apostolic Church?" Andrew Murray replied:

> Basing my views on scripture, I do *not* believe that miracles and the other gifts of the Spirit were limited to the time of the primitive Church, nor that their object was to establish the foundation of Christianity and then disappear by God's withdrawal of them . . . . The entire scriptures declare that these graces will be granted according to the measure of the Spirit and of faith.[12]

He further dismisses the idea that such a particularized presence of the hand of God was necessary only in the early days of Christianity:

> Ah, no! What about the power of heathenism even today wherever the gospel seeks to combat it, even in our *modern* society, and in the midst of the ignorance and unbelief which reigns even in the Christian nations.[13]

It is one of the amazing conceits of the flesh that from time to time creeps into the Church. We are so much better now than in more primitive times that it is enough to have a written Word of God without the kind of divine presence recorded *in* that written Word.

With such ideas we shut ourselves off from God's present benefits. C.H. Spurgeon comments on Psalm 103:2:

> Ought we not to look upon our own history as being at least as full of God, as full of His goodness and of His truth, as much a proof of His faithfulness and veracity, as the lives of any of the saints who have gone before? We do our Lord an injustice when we suppose that He wrought all His mighty acts, and showed Himself strong for those in the early time, but doth not perform wonders or lay bare His arm for the saints who are now upon the earth. Let us review our own lives. Surely in these we may discover some happy incidents, refreshing to ourselves and glorifying to our God. Have you had no *deliverances*? Have you passed through no rivers, supported by the divine presence? Have you walked through no fires unharmed? Have you had no *manifestations*? Have you had no choice favours? . . . Surely the goodness of God has been the same to us as to the saints of old.[14]

Bible Deism

Frankly, there is abroad in the world today, and very strongly present in conservative religious circles, a position which we may aptly characterize as "Bible Deism." Classical Deism, associated with the extreme rationalism of the sixteenth and eighteenth centuries, held that God created His world complete and perfect and went away leaving man to his own devices. There was no individualized intervention in the lives of human beings: no miracle. Now "Bible Deism" holds, similarly, that God gave man the Bible and then went away leaving him to his own devices with it, and no individualized communication through the Bible or otherwise.

Bible Deism is very like the Sadducean doctrine current in the time of Jesus and Paul—that God finished speaking when He was done speaking with Moses, so that no alleged communications *via* angels or spirits could possibly be valid. It will be recalled that Paul, himself a Pharisee, and having actually dealt with angels and spirits, was able to divide his accusers upon one occasion and defuse a bad situation by speaking of the resurrection, which the Pharisees but not the Sadducees accepted. The Pharisees then, to make a point important to them, sided with Paul: "We find no evil in this man: but if a spirit or an angel hath spoken to him, let us not fight against God" (Acts 23:9). Far too many who intend to honor the Bible adopt, similarly to the Sadducees, an unbiblical teaching about God's relationship to His children.

From the pastoral point of view, one of the greatest harms we can do to those under our care is to convince them that God is not going to meet them personally in their experience, or that He is *really* doing so only if we approve of what is happening. If our gospel does not free the individual up for a unique life of spiritual adventure in living with God daily, we simply have not entered into the Good News which Jesus brought. The Lord does run *His* Church, and all our efforts must be directed toward fostering each person's individual adventure with Him. We can trust Him, and we cannot trust anything else, not even the sterling soundness and sobriety of our own "faith and practice." If we trust anything else, we will cause our charges to trust something else, and may have, at best, proper spiritual corpses to fill our pews. We should shudder before the words of Jesus to ministers of His day: "You travel about on sea and land to make one proselyte; and when he becomes one, you make him twice as much a son of hell as yourselves" (Matt. 23:15, *NASB*).

And yet there *are* dangers. The adventure can get disastrously out of hand. We know that people do go off the deep end. And the problem is one which must be addressed. After gravely warning that death and disaster *also* may come from going off the *shallow* end, what must be done from the pastoral point of view is to lead people into an understanding of the voice of God and how it works in their lives. Most importantly and right at the outset they must be made to see that recognizing the guidance of God is something which *must be learned through a course of personal experience and experimentation.* Especially, if they do not expect God to speak to them, they must be encouraged to do so; and we may even at the outset have to identify the voice of God for them and instruct them on how to respond. Those who are older in The Way should be prepared to do this by their own experience.

How wonderful that Eli recognized what was happening to young Samuel and could tell him what to do to begin his lifelong conversational walk with God (1 Sam. 3)! It might well have been years, in the prevailing circumstances, before Samuel would have found his way. We must not foolishly assume that if God speaks, one automatically knows what is happening and who is talking. If Samuel did not know, surely many others also would not.

How wonderful that Abraham could assure his puzzled servant (Gen. 24:1-7) of God's guidance back to the city of Nahor to find a wife for Isaac! How wonderful that the servant could come to an utterly new understanding of God because he *was* experientially guided—and indeed, guided into knowledge of guidance itself!

The Priority of the Voice

Knowledge and experience of guidance teaches us many things that can keep us from harm and from harming others in our spiritual adventure of life in God's Kingdom. And one of the most important things we learn is *the superiority of the voice* over the other epiphanies—however the "voice" may come, even within the silence of our own minds. This superiority lies in two things: (1) the clarity of its cognitive content, and (2) the advanced spiritual condition of those who can hear and receive it.

In Numbers 12 we find Aaron and Miriam, brother and sister of Moses, criticizing him because he had married a

Cushite woman. Really, they were jealous of the way God spoke to Moses; "Has the Lord indeed spoken only through Moses? Has He not spoken through us as well?" (v. 2, *NASB*). Now this apparently was no problem with Moses. He wanted everyone to prophesy (Num. 11:29), and he was a very humble man. But the Lord did not disregard it, and called the three of them into the meeting tent. He then came down in a cloud and called Aaron and Miriam forward: "Hear now My words: If there is a prophet among you, I the Lord shall make Myself known to him in a vision. I shall speak with him in a dream. Not so, with My servant Moses, He is faithful in all My household; with him I speak mouth to mouth, even openly, and not in dark sayings, and he beholds the form of the Lord. Why then were you not afraid to speak against My servant, against Moses?" (Num. 12:6-8, *NASB*).

"Not in dark sayings." This phrasing is important for our contemporary understanding of God's guidance. "Dark" sayings are, of course, *obscure,* barely intelligible sayings. We do not know for sure what they mean. Many who claim to speak for God refer to their visions, dreams, and other unusual phenomena—or to their vague impressions or feelings—but with no clear, sane meaning. This does not mean that they are not truly spoken to. But Moses was spoken to directly—mouth to mouth, or *conversationally.* His meaning when he spoke for God was, therefore, always specific, precise, and clear.

We notice as we proceed on through Bible history that the greater the maturity, the greater the cognitive clarity of the message and the lesser is the role played by dreams, visions and other "strange" phenomena in the process of communication. Of course we cannot argue conclusively from silence, but we notice in the lives of New Testament personalities—and especially including that of Jesus Himself—a great preponderance of strictly spiritual communications between God and man. Visions, dreams, and angels continue to play a role—as I think they do today; but it may not be too much to say that where these were the main, as opposed to occasional, means of interaction between God and man, these indicate a less developed spiritual life in the individual and in the church group.

We turn again to the words of E. Stanley Jones, who so greatly believed in and practiced interaction with divine guidance throughout his life:

> God cannot guide you in any way that is not Christlike. Jesus was supreme sanity. There was nothing psychopathic about Him. He went off into no visions, no dreams. He got His guidance through prayer as you and I do. That is, He got His guidance when in control of His faculties, and not when out of control as in dreams. I do not say that God may not guide through a vision or dream; but if He does, it will be very seldom, and it will be because He cannot get hold of our normal mental processes to guide them. For God is found most clearly and beneficially in the normal rather than in the abnormal. And Jesus is the Normal, for He is the Norm.[15]

More Is Less

I believe that the predominance of the spectacular encounter does, in general, go along with the *less* mature levels of the spirit—though the mere absence of such spectacular events is not to be taken as indicating great spiritual development, for it is also consistent with utter deadness, and it is, of course, well that this should be so. The spectacular encounters are obscure in their meaning, in their cognitive content. This protects us. For in general, knowledge tends to be destructive when not held in a mature personality thoroughly permeated by love and humility. Few things are more terrifying in the spiritual realm than those who *absolutely know,* but are in fact unloving, hostile, proud, superstitious, and fearful. That Aaron and Miriam could be jealous of Moses is a certain indication that God could never trust them with the kind of knowledge He gave freely to Moses. That Moses was untroubled by their attack, and glad to share the prophetic ministry just as surely indicated that he could be trusted with knowledge.

The spectacular is sought because of childishness. Children love the spectacular, and show themselves as children by seeking it, running heedlessly after it. And it may be given by God—may be necessary—because of our denseness or our hardheartedness. However, it is *never* to be taken as a mark of spiritual superiority; and those who are advanced in The Way of Christ will—if spectacular things come to them—never lightly discuss them or, especially, invoke them to prove that they are right.

God in His mercy often speaks to us, but obscurely, in order to allow us the room and time needed to respond—to let us know that we indeed are being addressed, but to stretch us out in growth in order to receive the message. Perhaps we often think: "Well, God, why don't you just come out and say it? Tell me how to live." But this is usually said in a context of our own wrong ideas about how that would work out. There is a problem of reworking our minds so that God's glory and our interests are truly appreciated and understood. We may, like Isaiah, cry out for God to rend the heavens, come out of hiding, and stand there before us telling us what to do (Isa. 64:1). But we do not *really* understand what it is we are asking for, and it probably would literally kill us or destroy our minds if it happened. So God in His mercy continues to approach us obliquely, in one way and another, even until that time when we can safely know Him as He now knows us (1 Cor. 13:12).

So it is natural and right that the word comes to us in forms with which we must struggle. In the process of struggling we grow to the point where we can appropriate and assimilate the content of truth as it becomes clear. It is one of the oldest and most common stories of human life that in its most important moments we have little more than the foggiest idea of what it is we are doing and saying. Did you know what was happening when you got married or brought a child into this world? In some vague sense you did, but you also had very little idea of what it *meant*. Had you at the time appreciated all that it meant, you probably would not have had the courage to proceed, and you then would have missed all the great good that was to come to you.

Thus in religion also we come very slowly to appreciate what is happening to us. James and John came to Jesus and said, in effect, "Lord, when you become King we want to be your Secretary of State and Secretary of the Treasury." He replied: "You do not know what you are asking. Can you drink the cup that I will drink of, be baptized with my baptism?" With great assurance they replied: "Oh yes, Lord, we are able to do that; bring it on" (Mark 10:37-39). But they had no idea. And it turned out that by the Lord's mercy they *were* able to drink His cup and take His baptism. They were prepared when the time came. James was the first one of the apostles to be martyred. According to tradition, John was boiled in oil, and we know that he was exiled on the barren island of Patmos where he experienced the Revelation of Jesus Christ in a form utterly new to all his previous experience. These things were not what they had in mind, by any means, but they did very well because God was with them. They grew to the vision and the task as they stepped forward in faith. They lived and they finally died as the friends and co-laborers of Jesus and His Father and theirs.

Bob Mumford, discussing the spectacular forms of guidance, remarks:

> Signs are given to us, because God meets us on

the level where we operate . . . . In guidance, when God shows us a sign, it doesn't mean we've received the final answer. A sign means we're on the way. On the highway we may pass a sign saying, "New York: 100 miles." The sign doesn't mean we've reached New York, but it tells us we're on the right road.[16]

But, on the other hand, he continues:

God wants to bring us beyond the point where we need signs to discern His guiding hand. Satan cannot counterfeit the peace of God or the love of God dwelling in us. When Christ's abiding presence becomes our guide, then guidance becomes an almost unconscious response to the gentle moving of His Holy Spirit within us.[17]

How glad I am that history was finally ready to be addressed in the still small voice of Jesus! That God left the spectacular forms which were necessary—and perhaps still are necessary for some purposes—and came to deal with us even by the whispers of God's Spirit. Few of us would really know what to do if the great God came down in full splendor and stood before us. In the language of Job, "Lo, these are but the outskirts of his ways; and how small a whisper do we hear of him! But the thunder of his power who can understand?" (Job 26:14, *RSV*). The Incarnate Son comes without strife, so gentle that His voice is not to be heard above the street noise (Matt. 12:19). It is because of this that the Gentiles trust in His name. I am so thankful for the quiet written Word, for the history and presence of the Church of the Lamb of God, for the lives of the saints, and for the tireless, still conquests of the Spirit of God. These approach me. These I can approach, and through them approach God while He safely draws nigh to me.

The rivals of the Voice—still and small, still and within—are necessary and have their place, then. But once we get beyond the need to have "big things" happening to reassure ourselves that somehow we are right and alright—and possibly that others are not—then we begin to understand and rejoice that, as Jesus so clearly lived and taught, the life of the Kingdom is the "inner" life. Then we begin to understand that God's whole purpose is to bring us to the point where He can walk with us quietly, calmly, constantly, leaving us space to grow, to be His (often fumbling) co-laborers, to have some distance from Him, and *yet* be united with Him because we have been conformed to the image of His Son. We bear the family resemblance.

Even at the merely human level one of the highest forms of communication is that kind of communion in which no overt communication is needed or wanted. What are we to make of a poet who says, "Drink to me only with thine eyes, and I'll but pledge with mine"? We must say that he has touched upon an element of that to which God would finally bring us in the communion with Him which is a union sometimes beyond communication, and in a constant life before Him in this world and the next. There is a silence which says all.

> Love culminates in bliss when it doth reach
> A white, unflickering, fear-consuming glow;
> And, knowing it is known as it doth know,
> Needs no assuring word or soothing speech.
> It craves but silent nearness, so to rest,
> No sound, no movement, love not heard but felt,
> Longer and longer still, till time should melt.
> A snow-flake on the eternal ocean's breast.
>
> Have moments of this silence starred thy past,

Made memory a glory-haunted place,
Taught all the joy that mortal ken can trace?

By greater light 'tis but a shadow cast:—
So shall the Lord thy God rejoice o'er thee,
And in His love will rest, and silent be.[18]

Questions

1. What is *your* reaction to the Virginia Lively story? Why?

2. What are the six ways mentioned in this chapter in which people are addressed by God within the biblical record?

3. "The spirit of man is the candle of the Lord." Explain.

4. It is very common to hear religious leaders speak of "having a *personal relationship* with God (through Jesus Christ)." In your opinion, can such a "personal relationship" make sense without God speaking directly to that individual? Explain.

5. As a means of God's communication, the voice is superior for two reasons. What are they?

6. What is "Bible Deism"? Do you know any practitioners?

7. What is meant by "more is less"? Do you agree?

Notes

1. *Guideposts* magazine letter number 117-2, December, 1982.
2. Mortimer J. Adler, *The Angels and Us* (New York: Macmillan Publishing Company, Inc., 1982), preface.
3. Gustave Oehler, *Technology of the Old Testament* (Grand Rapids: Zondervan Publishing Co., n.d.), p. 143.
4. Ibid.
5. Samuel Shoemaker, *With the Holy Spirit and with Fire* (New York: Harper and Row Publishers, Inc., 1960), p. 27.
6. Russ Johnston, *How to Know the Will of God* (Colorado Springs: NavPress, 1971), p. 13.
7. Thomas Goodwin, *The Vanity of Thoughts* and *Let Patience Have Its Perfect Way* (Wilmington: Classic-A-Month Books, 1964), p. 4.
8. Garry Friesen, *Decision Making and the Will of God* (Portland, OR: Multnomah Press, 1980), p. 129.
9. Ibid., p. 144.
10. Rosalind Rinker, *Prayer: Conversing with God* (Grand Rapids: Zondervan Publishing House, 1959), p. 17 (italics added).
11. Ibid., p. 19.
12. Leona Choy, *Andrew Murray: Apostle of Abiding Love* (Ft. Washington, PA: Christian Literature Crusade, 1978), pp. 152-153.
13. Ibid.
14. Charles H. Spurgeon, *Morning by Morning* (London: Passmore and Alabaster, 1865), p. 191.
15. E. Stanley Jones, *The Way* (Nashville: Abingdon-Cokesbury Press, 1946), p. 283.
16. Bob Mumford, *Take Another Look at Guidance: Discerning the Will of God* (Plainfield, NJ: Logos International, 1971), pp. 140-141.
17. Ibid.
18. Sonnet, by Frances Ridley Havergal.

CHAPTER 6

THE WORD OF GOD AND THE RULE OF GOD

By the word of the Lord the heavens were made, and all their host by the breath of his mouth (Psalm 33:6, RSV*).*

He gives an order; his word flashes to earth: to spread snow like a blanket, to strew hoarfrost like ashes (Psalm 147:15-16, JB*).*

Then they called to Yahweh in their trouble and he rescued them from their sufferings; sending his word and curing them, he snatched them from the Pit (Psalm 107:19-20, JB*).*

Where the word of a king is, there is power (Ecclesiastes 8:4).

He is known to us only as "a certain centurion" (Luke 7:2). He was a Gentile, a Roman soldier of considerable rank: top man, we may assume, in the area of Capernaum. He also was a good governor who sacrificed his goods to help his subjects (Luke 7:5), and a good man who loved his servant, sick to the point of death. And he was humble. But these things were not what impressed Jesus.

What impressed Jesus was the quality and magnitude of the man's faith. He seemed to understand from his own experience of authority *how* Jesus accomplished what He did, and therefore had complete trust in His power. In a manner almost casual and offhand he said to Jesus: "Don't trouble yourself, sir! I'm not important enough for you to come into my house—I didn't think I was fit to come to you in person. Just give the order, please, and my servant will recover. I am used to working under orders and I have soldiers under me. I can say to one, 'Go,' and he goes, or I can say to another, 'Come here,' and he comes; or I can say to my slave, 'Do this job,' and he does it" (Luke 7:6-8, *Phillips*).

Jesus looked at this man with astonishment. Turning to the group following along after Him He then said, "I have never found faith like this anywhere, even in Israel" (v. 9, *Phillips*). What! Did not John the Baptist have greater faith? Did not those who heralded and welcomed the child Jesus as the Messiah? Did not His own family and followers have greater faith than this Gentile soldier? Apparently not.

Great strength is evidenced by the ease of its workings. As "the quality of mercy is not strained," so also with faith. Most of what we think we see as the struggle *of* faith is really the struggle to act *as if* we had faith when in fact we do not. We must return to this centurion later. He has much to teach us about faith and about its dependence upon a proper understanding of the word of God.

Words and the Word

God *created,* God *rules,* God *redeems* through the instrumentality of His word. God creating, God ruling,

God redeeming *is* His word. This is the single basic truth about the overall relationship which He has to His creatures. We see in it the all-encompassing mediatorship of the Word. If we would understand God's personal relationship to us, including guidance provided to our individual lives, we must understand what in general the word of God is, and how both the Son of God and the Bible are the Word of God.

So we must think in depth about what words are. If you find a word written on a wall, or simply overhear one spoken, you cannot tell *whose* word it is. Its ownership does not reside within itself, considered merely as a mark or sound. *My* word is not just *a* word. It is me speaking or me writing. Even my name written on a check ever so clearly is not *my* word, not my "signature" if *I* did not write it and thereby express my *self—my* thoughts and *my* intentions.

What is essential to the word of a person is the meaning given to it by them; that is, what thought, feeling, or action *they* associate with it and hope to convey to others. Through our words we give to others a "piece of our mind," and through their words we may know their thoughts and feelings and share in their very lives.

Through words, soul impacts soul with the force of planets in collision. As marks or sounds alone, words, of course, are nothing. It is their mental side, their spiritual force, which gives them their immense power. If we do not understand Spanish or Greek we may hear the sounds but they have little or no effect because they are without meaning for us.

The power of the word lies finally in the personality which it conveys. Children learn to say: "Sticks and stones may break my bones, but words can never hurt me." Adults teach them to say this in order to assuage the terrible pain which really is inflicted upon them by the words of their playmates.

How deeply children hurt from words! The schoolyard

and playroom become a chamber of horrors where little ones are drawn and quartered and left permanently crippled and scarred by malicious or mindless chatter and prattle. Jesus saw this, no doubt, for *He* had eyes which saw; and He also saw adults ravaging the souls of little children with their words. Surely it was only His sense of the damage thus done which made Him say: "But whoso shall offend one of these little ones which believe in me, it were better for him that a millstone were hanged about his neck, and that he were drowned in the depth of the sea" (Matt. 18:6).

The true view of the power of words is wisely given in the book of Proverbs: "Death and life are in the power of the tongue " (18:21)."A soft tongue may break down solid bone" (25:15, *NEB*). "The tongue that soothes is a tree of life; the barbed tongue, a breaker of hearts" (15:4, *JB*).

This theme is carried into the New Testament. James remarks that the tongue is "only a tiny part of the body, but it can proudly claim that it does great things. Think how small a flame can set fire to a huge forest" (Jas. 3:5, *JB*). Jesus our Lord regarded words as a direct revelation of the state of the soul: "By your words you shall be justified, and by your words you shall be condemned" (Matt. 12:37, *NASB*).

Words As Spiritual Forces

We cannot afford to overlook the spiritual nature of words. Spirit is disembodied force, or force which works independently of physical or bodily forces. We are most clearly presented with spirit as the force which belongs to thought and intention—although it reaches far beyond these, as we are acquainted with them, and ultimately serves as the foundation of all reality.

The view of words as spiritual forces is one common both to Scripture and to pagan philosophers. Jesus said to His followers on an occasion where they were putting too much weight upon the material realm: "It is the spirit that gives life, the flesh has nothing to offer. The words I have spoken to you are spirit and they are life" (John 6:23, *JB*). This meant—in accordance with what we have just said about the nature of words—that through His words Jesus imparted Himself and in some measure imbued those who received His words with the powers of God's sovereign rule. They "tasted the good word of God, and the powers of the world to come" (Heb. 6:5). This power imparted is seen in His later explanation: "If you abide in Me, and My words abide in you, ask whatever you wish, and it shall be done for you" (John 15:7, *NASB*).

Plato, the great philosopher of ancient Greece, also spiritualizes words by treating thought itself as an inner "conversation" which the soul holds with itself.[1] In thus treating thought as a language—hence as words, but words hidden away in the non-physical realm—he sets a pattern which many thinkers follow up to the present day. Saint Augustine carried that tradition on, joining it to Christian thought, in saying that "he who thinks speaks in his heart." He explicitly founds his view in part upon Gospel passages such as Matthew 9:2-4, where "certain of the scribes *said within themselves*. This man blasphemeth."[2] (See also Luke 12:17.)

The word, as person speaking, is therefore to be understood as a *spiritual* power, whether of man or of God or of other personal agency, whether for evil or for good. It is the power of the person who speaks. It is precisely in this realm that God seeks for those who would worship Him "in spirit and in truth" (John 4:23). He desires truth in the "inward parts," and "in the hidden part thou shalt make me to know wisdom" (Ps. 51:6).

William Penn says, with the characteristically Quaker emphasis:

> For the more mental our worship the more adequate to the nature of God; the more silent, the more suitable to the language of a spirit.

> Words are for others, not for ourselves: nor for God who hears not as bodies do; but as spirits should. If we would know this dialect we must learn of the divine principle in us. As we hear the dictates of that, so does God hear us.[3]

The word of God, when no further qualification is added, *is God speaking, God communicating.*

When God speaks He expresses His mind. All expressions of His mind are "words" of God. This is true whether the specific instrumentality is *external* to the human mind—as in natural phenomena (Ps. 19:1-4), or other human beings, or in the incarnate Christ *(Logos),* or in the Bible—or *internal* to the human mind, in its own thoughts, intents, and feelings. His kingdom rule over all things, including the affairs of mankind, is carried out through His word thus understood.

A Kingdom of Words

Humanity is under constant temptation to think of the universe as a place in which there are only certain mechanical relationships between things, and to think of the blind forces pushing and pulling among physical objects as *the* way in which all things relate to one another. This is the naturalistic outlook discussed in an earlier chapter. But such a view can never understand the affairs of men, and much less still can it understand the religious life. The religious life and the religious outlook on the universe—and of course we are especially concerned with that religious outlook which is identifiable with the mind of Christ and with life in His steps—is one which sees the universe as a *kingdom.* And a kingdom does not work merely by pushes and pulls. It essentially works by communication of thoughts and intentions.

This is a point which we cannot afford to miss. Some of our greatest problems in understanding and entering into life in the Kingdom of God come from inadequate appreciation of how that kingdom works by communication: by the speaking of words or the use of words. We turn now to the Scriptures to illustrate ways in which the speaking of a word works in the Kingdom of God.

Let us begin with the first chapter of the first book in the Bible where we find an account of the *creation* of the heavens and the earth. We are told that in the beginning God created the heavens and the earth. And how did He do it? By speaking. By a sequence of directly *creative words.* It should not come as a surprise, given what the advance of knowledge has brought to light about the physical universe, that the first creative act of God (Gen. 1:3) was to create *light,* a form of energy. And how did He create light? He *said,* "Let there be light." We recall that God speaking—the word of God—is simply the expression of His mind. Through the expression of His mind, then, He created light; and, conversely, the creation of light is itself to be viewed as an expression of the mind of God.

Is it possible to illuminate these passages from Genesis in some small measure by reflecting on how *we* create? You yourself may express your mind through creation and in what you create. Generally, if you do so, you will have to do *more* than just "speak." For example, if you are to create a bouquet of flowers or a cake, you cannot just say: "Let there be flowers!" or "Let there be angelfood cake!"

Here we have before us the very essence and meaning of finitude. Finitude means limitation or *restriction.* You and I are under some restrictions regarding how we can make a cake. We must work with and through the eggs and the flour and the sugar and the heat of the oven and the time. We must adapt ourselves and our actions to their natures. One cannot make a silk purse from a sow's ear, as the saying goes—nor a sow's ear from a silk purse. The structures within the substances with which we deal dictate the order in our actions.

But finally the cake comes forth, if we know what we are doing, and it is an expression of our self, our thoughts and feelings and intentions. The husband who only eats the cake without comment has not got that point. He must find it good and *say* so. Better yet, he must say, in so many words, "How good *of you* to make this cake for me!"

At a still more creative level of human life we have what are called *inventions.* Normally the cake will be thought of as just something nice which you were able to produce by following the directions or knowing how to make it. But if a person conceives of a new type of engine or clothing or communicative device, *that* is an "invention." It too is an expression of the mind of its creator. Hence we glorify inventors and authors as special kinds of persons. Here, also, thought—the internal "word"—governs events in the material world. But here also it works under restrictions. One cannot create a jet engine just by saying or thinking, "Let there be a jet engine!"

But this is not yet the end of human powers of creation. There is one domain where the human mind but "speaks" and it is done. That is in the voluntary motions of the body, of the hands, the feet, the face, and in extended ranges of our inward thoughts. God, of course, is *always* able to speak and to create thereby without "going through channels," without working under restrictions—though He does not always choose to do so. This constitutes His infinity. Within a certain range—very narrow, in contrast to God's—we too have been given in our own "natural" powers a similarly unrestricted ability. In the realm of our familiar finitude we learn how to do things. We learn how to break the eggs and how to stir the batter, how to steer the automobile and put on the brakes. But we do not *know how* to move our finger or our tongue or our foot. Here there are no "channels" to go through in the normal case. The action is immediate, and in our conscious processes there is no "how" about it. The thought, the intent is there, and the body, with all of the physical intricacies involved, just moves.

We, similarly, know how to interpret a passage of

Scripture or how to read music or how to solve a crossword puzzle or dissect an argument from the editorial page of the newspaper. There is, accordingly, a "how to" across broad ranges of the mental life also. But at a certain point you *directly* think of certain things or decide on a course of action. If I ask you to think of a kitten, you do so with no *how to.* To ask, under normal circumstances, "How shall I think of a kitten?" makes no more sense than to ask, "How shall I move my little finger?"

Here in this restricted range of direct action, God has given us an immediate power which, so far as our conscious governance is concerned, is as immediately creative as His own. This is what it means for us to have *life.* And, in this life given, He even permits us to use our little power to oppose Him, even to hate Him, in order that our compliance, if and when it comes, might be the free and intelligent response of a person to a person.

Probably there is no very clear boundary, or at least not a clear understanding of the boundary, between what we can influence directly by our thoughts and intents and what we cannot. We are astonished at great feats of "will power"; and if you can bend nails or spoons by "mental force"—or if you can even make it seem that you are doing so—you will certainly be invited to appear on television talk shows. Biofeedback techniques have proven that by the immediate direction of our thoughts and our imagery we can control the rate of our heartbeat and the level of our blood pressure. But the creative word of God is without limitation, unless such limitation is purposely adopted by God Himself. He says, "Let there be light," and there *is* light—just as you intend your arm to rise and it rises.

Our own experience of thought, or of the "inner word," translating itself into creation is absolutely vital to our understanding of God's rule *through* His word. Returning to Genesis 1 we see God continuing to create by the direct action of His word upon the results of His *first* creative word—which produced light or energy from itself alone, energy which we now know to be the substance of matter. Thus in verse 6, "Let there be a firmament in the midst of the waters, and let it divide the waters from the waters." In verse 9, "Let the waters under the heaven be gathered together." He spoke and thereby formed these specific things into existence. Verse 14: "Let there be lights in the firmament of the heaven." Verse 20: "And God said, Let the waters bring forth abundantly the moving creature that hath life." Verse 24: "God said, Let the earth bring forth." Verse 26: "And God said, Let us make man in our image."

In all these cases, as God spoke, the object concerned came into existence—whether in an instant or over a more or less extended period of time does not matter—just as your hand goes up in response to your thought and intent. *That* is the creative power of the word of God.

The thought, the mind, the word of God continues its presence in the created universe as *upholding* word. "Lasting to eternity, your word, Yahweh, unchanging in the heavens: your faithfulness lasts age after age; you founded the earth to endure. Creation is maintained by your rulings, since all things are your servants" (Ps. 119:89-91, *JB*).

Natural laws are God's thoughts as to how the world should run. Because of this, as the Christian philosopher George Berkeley has said, echoing Psalm 19, "God Himself speaks every day and in every place to the eyes of all men."[4] The events in the visible, material world—the unfolding of a rosebud, the germination of a seed, the conception and growth of a child, the evolution of galaxies—constitute a "visible language" manifesting not only a creative mind but, Berkeley continues,

> . . . a provident Governor, actually and intimately present, and attentive to all our interests and motions, who watches over our con-

> duct and takes care of our minutest actions and designs throughout the whole course of our lives, informing, admonishing, and directing incessantly, in a most evident and sensible manner.[5]

The Word of God As the Son of God

This "visible language," this "Word," present as the upholding order of the universe, "was in the world, and the world was made through Him, and the world did not know Him. He came to His own, and those who were His own did not receive Him" (John 1:10-11, *NASB*). The redemptive entry of God upon the human scene was therefore no intrusion into foreign territory, but into "His own"—a focusing into the finite form of a human personality of that divine thought which is the order of all creation. He, as the ancient prayer says, "did not abhor the Virgin's womb," for therein as always the control panel of the whole universe lay ready to hand, though He refrained from all but a very selective use of it. The seeming paradox of the incarnation is that Christ's in-fleshment *really* was no imposed restriction, but was the supreme exercise of the supreme power, as the end of human history will make abundantly clear: "Here is my servant, whom I have chosen, my beloved, on whom my favour rests; I will put my Spirit upon him, and he will proclaim judgement among the nations. He will not strive, he will not shout, nor will his voice be heard in the streets. He will not snap off the broken reed, nor snuff out the smouldering wick, until he leads justice on to victory. In him the nations shall place their hope" (Matt. 12:18-21, *NEB*).

The story of the New Testament is the story of increasing understanding of who Jesus was. Those among whom He was reared said, "This is Mary and Joseph's boy. We know him." His own disciples thought He might be Elijah or one of the old prophets risen from the dead. In a flash of divine revelation, Peter announced, as Jesus quizzed them on His identity: "Thou art the Christ" (Matt. 16:16)! Only in the later parts of the New Testament does there emerge the concept of Jesus as in fact a *cosmic* Christ, spanning all geographical and ethnic differences, but also, as we have seen, the "glue" of the universe (Col. 1:17), upholding all things by the *word* of His power (Heb. 1:3)—or, as the *Jerusalem Bible* translates it, "Sustaining the universe by his powerful command—the "Alpha and Omega" of the book of *Revelation,* the "Faithful and True," "The Word of God" leading the armies of heaven. "the King of Kings and Lord of Lords" (Rev. 19:11-16).

In all of its manifestations in nature and in the incarnate Christ, the word of God is characterized by overwhelming power. It is the awareness of this power that brings the prophet Isaiah to contrast the thoughts of man with the thoughts of God—which in their expression are the words of God. Mere human thoughts, though efficacious within their appointed range, are as far below the power of God's thoughts (and words) as the earth is below the heavens (Isa. 55:7-9). With a force comparable to the forces of nature—the rain and seed bringing forth plants, seed and bread to nourish the hungry (v. 10)—"So shall My word be which goes forth from My mouth; it shall not return to Me empty, without accomplishing what I desire, and without succeeding in the matter for which I sent it" (v. 11, *NASB*).

The *unity* of the natural order and God's redemptive community under the word of God is seen in Psalm 29. Here the behavior of the waters and of the forests are attributed to the voice of the Lord. "The voice of the Lord makes the deer to calve, and strips the forests bare" (v. 9, *NASB*). But while "the Lord sat as King at the flood," He also will "give strength to His people; the Lord will bless His people with peace" (vv. 10-11, *NASB*). This same unity is of course exhibited in the life of Jesus who could turn water into wine, calm the billowing waves with His word and walk upon them like a sidewalk, but who could also place the word of God's Kingdom rule into the hearts of men where it would bring forth fruit, "some an hundredfold, some sixty, some thirty" (Matt. 13:23).

This, then, is the word of God and the Son of God, and their unity in the governance of the cosmos. But to understand how the word of God is related to the *family* of God we must consider more closely the role of ordinary human words in ordinary human life. This may enable us to see how the power of the word of God operating among men differs from superstition, magic, and voodoo.

The Power in a Word

In the book of Ecclesiastes a wise man reflects in depth upon how human life and society work. Among other things he considers how kings or governments function. We read in Psalm 29 how the Lord sat as King at the flood, and we know that He is indeed King over all the earth and master of the most terrible of situations. But a king, contrary to what is often thought, does not rule simply by brute force.

The emperor Napoleon was upon one occasion about to use great force to subdue a certain population. But a wise lieutenant, one of his aides, said to him: "Monseigneur, one cannot *sit* upon bayonets." He understood that the use of mere force could not lead to a settled political rule. Truly, all government is in some significant degree by consent of the governed. No one can totally rule a people by force. Instead, the ruler rules by words, understandings, allegiances, and alliances.

The writer of Ecclesiastes, himself a king, was amazed at what the word of a king could do. He remarks: "Where the word of a king is, there is power: and who may say unto him, What doest thou?" (8:4). Take his authority away from him, and a king is like any other person. But when he is indeed kingly, his smallest word has awesome effects. Heads roll, nations prosper, cities burn, armies march. Those who oppose are crushed. Seeing clearly what occurs at the merely human level may help our faith to rise to an understanding of the power of the creative word of God.

Poets are in the business of seeing, and no poet has seen the power of an "official" human word from on high better than Dylan Thomas:

> The hand that signed the paper felled a city;
> Five sovereign fingers taxed the breath,
> Doubled the globe of dead and halved a country;
> These five kings did a king to death.
>
> The mighty hand leads to a sleeping shoulder,
> The finger joints are cramped with chalk;
> A goose's quill has put an end to murder
> That put an end to talk.
>
> The hand that signed the treaty bred a fever,
> And famine grew, and locusts came;
> Great is the hand that holds dominion over
> Man by a scribbled name.
>
> The five kings count the dead but do not soften
> The crusted wound nor pat the brow;
> An hand rules pity as a hand rules heaven;
> Hands have no tears to flow.[6]

Words in the Kingdom of God

Now as we turn to the Kingdom of God with an understanding that it *is* precisely a kingdom, and that it too, therefore, in a large measure works by words, events from the life of Jesus upon earth are easier to appreciate and enter into.

At the opening of this chapter we met "a certain centurion" who knew how words of authority work. He had implicit faith in Jesus, not, it seems, on a religious basis but from his quite secular knowledge of the power of authoritative words. So far as one can tell from the story, he did not have any special degree of faith in God, though he was a good man and respected the Jewish religion. He simply knew how authority worked, and he recognized that Jesus was working with authority to heal. When (as recorded in Matt. 8) Jesus entered into the city of Capernaum upon one occasion, this centurion came "beseeching him, and saying, Lord my servant lieth at home sick of the palsy, grievously tormented" (vv. 5-6). Palsy is paralysis, often accompanied with involuntary tremors. Without being asked, Jesus said, "I will come and heal him." Just like that! It was nothing extraordinary. We must remember, now, that for Jesus this was like saying, "I'll raise my hand."

The centurion was in a position to understand Jesus' response. He replied: "Lord, don't bother. I'm not worthy that you should come under my roof." This was both an act of humility and a courtesy on the part of the centurion. He knew that he was speaking to a Jew, and that a Jew did not like to come into the house of a Gentile lest he be defiled. So, in an act of courtesy: "You don't need to come. Just *speak the word only* and my servant shall be healed." Speak the word only? Yes, for where the word of a king is, there is power! This centurion understood it because he was, within his own arena, a "king" authorized to speak for a higher king, Caesar, and he therefore was able to recognize one who was clearly acting with the authority of a King.

In both scriptural accounts of his meeting with Jesus the centurion is allowed to explain fully *how he knows* that Jesus can just "speak the word only" and heal his servant: "For I am a man under authority, having soldiers under me: and I say to this man, Go, and he goeth; and to another Come, and he cometh; and to my servant, Do this, and he doeth it" (Matt. 8:9; compare Luke 7:8). What we have here is *experiential knowledge of the power of the word.* In a personal universe, the word directs actions and events. The centurion understood this, and Jesus marveled at his understanding: "Verily I say unto you, I have not found so great faith, no, not in Israel" (Matt. 8:10).

This is one of those points where our practical atheism may abruptly emerge. We are apt to find ourselves saying, "Things just aren't like that!" But what is it that is wrong? What is amiss with a universe in which reality responds to a word? What is wrong with a universe in which reality responds to thoughts and intentions? Surely we live in precisely such a universe, but our faith does not normally rise to it.

In part, no doubt, our skepticism about this personalistic framework is produced by the fact that we speak words which are seldom, if ever, accompanied by faith and authority, and such words of course do not have the effect on reality of words freighted with faith. Thus *our* experience, unlike the centurion's, hinders rather than helps our faith.

We must not miss the point here. For the centurion it was perfectly easy because he recognized that he was dealing with someone in high authority. He knew what authority was. He knew what it was to command an event. He knew that Jesus was doing the same kind of thing. So it was a simple matter for him to step into the situation. Where *he* had no authority—and thus could not himself say, "Be healed"—he yet could recognize the One who did have such authority, and he could in faith ask that person to use *His* authority to direct processes within the material universe, namely, the healing of his servant.

" 'But to prove to you that the Son of Man has authority on earth to forgive sins,'—he said to the paralytic—'get up, and pick up your bed and go off home.' And the man got up and went home. A feeling of awe came over the crowd when they saw this, and they praised God for giving such power to men" (Matt. 9:6-8, *JB*).

"Miracles of grace must be the seals of our ministry;

who can bestow them but the Spirit of God" (C.H. Spurgeon).[7]

From the biblical record we know that a powerful word such as Jesus spoke *has* been given unto man. In Numbers 20:8-12 we find a fascinating case study on this point. The situation is one where the Israelites, in their wilderness wanderings, are dying for lack of water. Moses' leadership is under violent criticism from his people. This drives him to prayer, as it ought, and God appears to him to tell him to *speak* to a rock which was close by "and it shall give forth his water, and thou shalt bring forth to them water out of the rock" (v. 8). But Moses took the rod which God had earlier given him as a sign and, with Aaron, called the people together: "Hear now, ye rebels; must we fetch you water out of this rock? And Moses lifted up his hand, and with his rod he smote the rock twice: and the water came out abundantly, and the congregation drank, and their [animals] also" (20:10-11).

So Moses smote the rock instead of speaking to it. God dealt sternly with him for his disobedience, not allowing him to cross into the land of promise "Because ye believed me not" (v. 12). But was it truly such a serious offense? Did it deserve such a strong reaction from God? And if so, why? Possibly Moses was attempting to answer those who criticized *his* power, or possibly he did not believe that merely speaking to a rock could break water out of it. Possibly he thought *he* had to bring forth the water by his own physical strength—"must *we* fetch you water out of this rock?" But the rock, we learn in 1 Corinthians 10, *was Christ.* Rocks—if what we have come to understand about the *logos* or word in nature is true—are things which well might respond to words spoken with the appropriate authority and vision of faith.

The transfer of the power of *God's* word to "ordinary" men was something which Jesus in His days of humility approached experimentally. *He* could exercise this power, but could He transfer it to his followers? That was the question they were facing.

So he commissioned His disciples to do what they had so often seen Him do, and sent them on their way: "Go, preach, saying, The kingdom of heaven is at hand. Heal the sick, cleanse the lepers, raise the dead, cast out devils: freely ye have received, freely give" (Matt. 10:7-8; compare Luke 9:1-10). This first experiment was with his twelve apostles only. When they returned and reported good success in acting in the power of God's word, the question then was: Can this transfer of God's power be extended even beyond these close followers to "ordinary" believers? This question remained, and so, according to Luke 10:1, Jesus sent out "other seventy also."

Now it seems to me to be a matter of great significance that these "other seventy" were not his closest associates—not, we might say, the best trained troops in the army of the Lord. Yet they too returned rejoicing in the knowledge that even demons were subject to them through the name of their Master (Luke 10:17). This seems to have had the effect of settling the mind of our Lord upon the extended incarnational plan of saving man. It was only at *this* point that Jesus saw Satan in defeat through the transfer of the word of God and its power to ordinary men who could then speak *with God* (Luke 10:17).

In this touching passage (Luke 10:21-23) Jesus seems positively gleeful as in no other scriptural passage. He "exulted in the Holy Spirit," as the *New English Bible* translates it. The Greek word *agalliaō* (v. 21) used here suggests the state of mind in which people may jump up and down with joy. Then he turned aside, perhaps, for a moment of thanks to his Father: "I praise Thee, O Father, Lord of heaven and earth, that Thou didst hide these things from the wise and intelligent and didst reveal them to babes. Yes, Father, for thus it was well-pleasing in Thy sight" (v. 21, *NASB*).

Under the vivid realization of the meaning of these

events He then informed His followers with assurance that His Father had turned everything over to Him—"All things have been handed over to Me by My Father"—and that He, Jesus Christ, was to be totally in charge of the revelation of the Father to humanity (v. 22, *NASB*). He then congratulated them on their good fortune in being able to witness what had happened as *ordinary* people succeeded in handling the power of God. Prophets and kings had longed to see this, but had not been able to (v. 23-24).

Thus did the kingdom rule of God *through* the actions and words of men reaffirm itself within the nation of Israel just before that kingdom was taken from it. Because of their failure to fulfill their divine appointment of being the light of the world, of showing the world how to live under God, Jesus said to the Israelites of His day: "Therefore I say to you, the kingdom of God will be taken away from you, and be given to a [people] producing the fruit of it" (Matt. 21:43, *NASB*). Not as if the Jews were to be excluded as individuals from exercise of the word of power in God's kingdom. Far from it. But it was no longer to be exclusively their role *as* Jews. The story of the transfer indicated by Jesus is precisely the story of the New Testament book of Acts.

Prayers, Action and Words

A proper understanding of the ways of the word of God among men in the kingdom rule of God illuminates something which has troubled many thoughtful students of the New Testament—that is, how rarely Jesus ever *prayed for* a need brought before Him. Rather, He would normally address it or perform some action in relation to it.

Such a case comes before us in Mark 9, where—while Jesus was on the Mount of Transfiguration—a man brought his child, possessed of a spirit that rendered him mute, to be healed. The disciples tried to cast the spirit out, but failed. When the Master arrived back on the scene He scolded His disciples for their inability (v. 19), and—after some conversation with the father about the child's condition and about the father's own faith—He cast the demon out. When the disciples then asked why they could not cast it out, for apparently they had previously had some success in such matters, Jesus replied: "This kind cannot come out by anything but prayer" (v. 29, *NASB*). And yet Jesus did *not* pray on this occasion. What is the explanation?

I believe we see illustrated here a principle to the effect that there are degrees of power in speaking the word of God and that prayer is necessary to heighten that power. Perhaps in some cases a direct word or action from God is required, and for that too we can only pray. But sometimes, on the other hand, *we should be* in a position to speak—to say on behalf of God and in the name of Christ how things are to be. To do this will be more or less difficult depending upon the specifics of the case. "This kind" will frequently differ from other kinds in other cases and call for other abilities, which we may or may not have available at the time. But I believe we are all to grow into this work in the measure appointed by God for us individually in our walk with the Lord and among His people.

Certainly in the biblical life led by the apostles of Jesus we see them speaking on behalf of God in the book of Acts and, less so, in the Gospels. They did not just pray to God for help. When Peter and John are confronted with the lame beggar as they enter the Temple in Acts 3, Peter commands the cripple *in the name of* Jesus Christ—on His behalf, that is—to rise up and walk. Then he *takes* him by the hand and *pulls* him to his feet (vv. 3-7). He does not kneel down and pray for him, nor does he pass on with a "We'll be praying for you!"

When dealing with Dorcas, the dead sister "full of good works and almsdeeds" (Acts 9:36), Peter put everyone out of the room (did he not learn this from Jesus—Matt. 9:25?) and, kneeling down, prayed. *Then* he faced the body and commanded her to arise, and Dorcas returned to life (Acts 9:40; perhaps Peter also learned from Elisha's practice in a similar situation, 2 Kings 4:32-35).

Paul at Lystra spoke the creative word of God to a lame man whose faith had been raised by hearing Paul preach. Paul loudly commanded the man, "Stand upright on thy feet." And he leaped and walked (Acts 14:10).

Of course there are multitudinous ways in which these matters might be misunderstood. They will be especially unsettling if we are already used to living our lives untouched by them and are convinced that they must have nothing to do with our faith or our service to God. If there is then a suggestion that *we* possibly should be healing the sick, casting out demons, raising the dead by our participation in the word and power of God, it may leave us baffled, rebellious, guilt-ridden.

Once after speaking in a certain church on accomplishing things through prayer, a woman confronted me in great agony and tears, with not a little anger. As we talked, it became clear that she had earlier believed that our prayers *could* actually make a difference in the course of events around us, and she had tried very hard to make it work in her life. But she had, for whatever reason, failed in the attempt and, obviously, that failure had left her feeling guilty and deeply hurt. To protect herself she had readjusted her faith—at least on the surface—to consist of believing the creeds, helping out at church, and being a good person generally, as that is commonly understood in our society. My words had reopened the old wounds and disturbed her hard-won peace. I have since come to understand that she was representative of many fine people who think well of Christ and would like to be His followers, but are convinced that the biblical mode of life in God's Kingdom just cannot be a reality for them.

On another occasion a woman, very devout, had been raised in a fellowship where stress was laid upon receiving a "second work of grace." She obviously had been driven to distraction in her frantic efforts to obtain this "deeper life" and cease being a second-class citizen among her religious friends. She too had "failed," and had recoiled into a life of mental assent to the truth about Jesus and some degree of effort for the local church with which she was associated. In this case I was only teaching about the joyous possibilities of life opened up by Jesus' invitation to enter His Kingdom, and how gladly that invitation was received by His hearers. But this woman was thrown into agony by talk of a life of *real* interaction with God in the manner of those described in the Old and New Testaments.

Now I cannot in these pages effectively deal with all of the issues involved in such cases, but there is one thing we can and must rest in: When we consider the life of participation in God's kingdom rule, we are not looking at anything which *we* must *make* happen. The extend of our obligation is to be willing to be made able. If we are to exercise the word and rule of God in ways regarded as spectacular by human beings, Jesus here as always is our model. And that means above all that there will be nothing forced or hysterical about it, and that we can count on God Himself to lead us into whatever we are to do. He will do this in such a way as is suitable to our lives and His calling for us. Beyond this we are only to remember the words of Jesus to His seventy friends on their return from their mission: "Nevertheless do not rejoice in this, that the spirits are subject to you, but rejoice that your names are recorded in heaven" (Luke 10:20, *NASB*).

With this firmly in mind, we turn to consider two final questions of this chapter: "How does a life in which one speaks the creative word of God differ from superstition, magic, and voodoo?" And, "What does the Bible have to do with the word of God as thus far discussed?"

Voodoo, Magic and Superstition

By "magic" we have in mind here not sleight of hand or mere trickery, but the attempt to influence the actual course of events, as distinct from their appearance, by manipulation of symbolisms or special substances such as effigies and incantations. Voodoo and witchcraft—sometimes lumped together as "black" magic—are the forms of magical practice most familiar to the Western mind. Satanism or demonism operates on yet a different principle, though it sometimes merges with magic. Magic and witchcraft are forms of *superstition,* which is belief that some action or substance or circumstance not logically or naturally related to a certain course of events does nonetheless, if correctly approached, influence the outcome of those events.

The word *superstition* itself is derived from words which mean "to stand over," as one might stand in wonder or amazement over something incomprehensible. The famous Connecticut Yankee in King Arthur's court, in Mark Twain's fictional portrayal, was able to lead the ignorant and generally superstitious people of ancient England to attribute unusual powers to his own actions, while he himself understood the natural causes of the events he manipulated.

Superstition, then, is belief in magic, and magic relies upon supposed causal influences not mediated through the natures of the things involved. Suppose someone says that they can throw you into great pain or even kill you by mutilating a doll-like effigy of you. This is a practice common in voodoo and other forms of witchcraft. I suspect that in some cases there is much more reality to the *effects claimed* than we might wish to credit from a common sense or scientific point of view. However, I do not believe that it is the mutilation of the doll or the incantations over it that produce the effects. Rather, the effects—where there are effects—come from the realm of the mind in a social context where a certain set of beliefs about voodoo or magical rituals are shared. The causation actually involved has nothing magical about it—as, indeed, *no* causation has—but is an entirely natural process through the prevailing psychosocial order.[8]

Now when we return to the ways in which Moses, Jesus, Peter, and Paul did the work of God, exercising His rule by speaking and acting with His word, there is neither magic nor superstition to be found; similarly for things which are much closer, possibly, to the life of the ordinary Christian today. Many of my readers who have difficulty conceptualizing the more spectacular episodes such as we have seen from Scriptures, still believe in the healing power of prayer and in the capacity of some individuals or some rituals practiced by the Church to minister in the healing of the body and in the supplying of other needs at a physical level. Why, now, is this not just more superstition?

The answer is that we do not believe the power concerned to reside in the words alone or in the rituals taken by themselves. Rather, the words and actions employed are simply the ways ordained in the nature of things, as established by God, for accomplishing the things in question. The specific condition of understanding, faith, love, and hope that is present in the person of those who work with the word of God is in its very nature connected with the effect to be brought about—to the nature of the human body or mind on the one hand, in the case of healing, and to the mind and Spirit of God on the other hand.

It is the nature of the material universe to be subject generally to an all-present, all-powerful, all-knowing divine Mind. This we see from the discussions in the first parts of the present chapter. This mind mediates between the word spoken by His servant on His behalf on the one hand, and the physical structure of the waves or rocks addressed, in the cases considered, or of the body or mind to be healed on the other. That is why Moses and Jesus, Peter and Paul, were *not* magicians.

Sometimes, however, I fear that we Christians *do* engage in truly superstitious usage of words and rituals, and especially when our activities are not an expression of any *understanding* of the connection between the consequence desired and our faith and union with God. A few years ago many Christians in the United States were caught up in a fad involving the phrase, "What you say is what you get." It was suggested that if you would just *affirm* what you wanted, you would get it. Further, if you *say* what you do not want—for example, voice something you are worried may happen—it will happen to you. Now this is superstition, in my opinion, to be placed alongside of those described by Jesus who in prayer use "vain repetitions," thinking "that they shall be heard for their much speaking" (Matt. 6:7). Possibly many people have nothing but superstition in their religious activities, with no understanding of the nature of God's Kingdom and how through His Word He rules in the affairs of men and, especially, within the family of the faithful. We each must search our own hearts on this matter. It does not have to be so.

The legalistic tendencies of the religious life also thrust us toward superstition. Legalism and superstition and magic are closely joined by their interest in *controlling* people and events. The legalist is forced toward superstitious behavior because in the interest of his laws he departs from the natural connections of life. Life does not come by law (Gal. 3:21), nor can law adequately depict or guide it. The law is letter, and "the letter killeth, but the spirit giveth life" (2 Cor. 3:6). The legalist is forced into merely symbolic behaviors which he superstitiously supposes has the good effects sought by him. Magic or superstition, for its part, places absolute emphasis upon doing everything "just right," which is the essence of legalism.

But walking in the power of God has nothing to do with superstition, as it has nothing to do with legalism or salvation through the law. In two different cases in the book of Acts the work of God was *mistaken* for magic by those without understanding. The first is that of Simon the Sorcerer in Acts 8. Beholding Peter and John conferring the Holy Spirit upon others, with the attendant manifestations, he offered money to them if they would but give him power to do the same (v. 18). Peter saw from this that Simon, though a "believer," did not have his heart right with God, and rebuked him severely for thinking "that the gift of God may be purchased with money" (v. 20).

In the nineteenth chapter of Acts we find a rather more humorous story. A traveling troop of Jewish exorcists, the seven sons of Sceva, saw the miracles worked by God with Paul and Paul with God. They listened to the *words* Paul used, mistaking them for incantations rather than intelligent, rational discourse within a society or kingdom. They then tried pronouncing the name "Jesus" over a person possessed of demons, saying "I command you by Jesus preached by Paul" (v. 13). The scriptural account of what then happened is so good that it must be simply quoted: "The evil spirit replied, 'Jesus I recognise, and I know who Paul is, but who are you?' and the man with the evil spirit hurled himself at them and overpowered first one and then another, and handled them so violently that they fled from that house naked and badly mauled" (vv. 15-16, *JB*).

This greatly impressed everyone in Ephesus, and the name "Lord Jesus" was held in great respect. Believers who had been using spells and practicing magic forsook such practices, realizing the great disparity between the realm of the magical and the Kingdom of God. They burned magic books worth fifty thousand pieces of silver, while for its part "the word of the Lord was growing mightily and prevailing" (v. 20, *NASB*).

We as followers of Christ are not to believe or act upon things that make no sense and which we only hope to manipulate for our own ends, no matter how good.

The Bible and the Word of God

Finally we come to the question of how we are to understand the relationship of the Bible to this word of God which we have just seen "growing mightily and prevailing" around Ephesus, and to that Word which is God, and which upholds the world.

The Bible is *one* of the results of God speaking. It is the *unique* written Word of God, and in conjunction with it God presently speaks to the devout heart ever anew. It is inerrant in its original form, and infallible in all of its forms for the purpose of guiding man into a saving relationship with God in His Kingdom; and it is thus infallible because God never leaves it alone.

The inerrancy of the original texts is rendered efficacious for the purposes of redemption only as that text and its present-day derivatives are constantly held within the eternal living Word. Inerrancy of the originals is not by itself a sufficient theory of biblical inspiration, because, as everyone knows, the Bible in our hand is not the original text. Inerrancy of the originals also does not guarantee sane and sound, much less error-free, interpretations. Our dependence *as* we read the Bible is upon God who now speaks in conjunction with it and our best efforts to understand it.

In the light of our discussions thus far it is clear that *the Bible is the written Word of God, but the word of God is not simply the Bible; and, the way we know that this is so is by paying attention to what the Bible says.*

If you take just the passages studied thus far and examine what they say about the word of God you will see that that word is much greater than the Bible, though inclusive of it. The Bible is the Word of God in its unique written form. But the Bible is not Jesus Christ, who is the living Word. And the Bible is not the word of God that is settled eternally in the heavens, as the psalmist says (Ps. 119:89), and expresses itself in the order of nature (Ps. 19:1-4). The Bible is not that word of God which in the book of Acts expanded and grew and multiplied (Acts 12:24). It is not the word which Jesus spoke of as being sown by the active speaking of the ministry (Matt. 13). But all of these are *God speaking.*

The Bible is the unique, infallible written Word of God. But the word of God is not just the Bible, and if we try to dignify the Bible by saying false things about it—that is, by simply *equating* the word of God with it—we do not dignify it. We betray its content by denying what it says about the nature of the word of God.

God reigns in His Kingdom through speaking. That "speaking" is reserved to Himself and those who work in union with Him. The Bible is a finite, written record of what the infinite, living God has spoken, and reliably fixes the boundaries of what He will ever say. It fixes those boundaries in principle, though it does not provide the detailed communications which God may have with individual believers.

The Bible has a special and irreplaceable role in redemption. We can refer any person to it with the assurance that if they will approach it openly, honestly, intelligently, and persistently, God will meet them through its pages and speak peace to their souls. This is assured to any person whose deepest self cries out:

> Beyond the sacred page I seek Thee, Lord;
> My spirit pants for Thee, O Living Word.[9]

Paul therefore instructed his protégé Timothy that "the sacred writings . . . are able to give you the wisdom that leads to salvation through faith which is in Christ Jesus. All Scripture is inspired by God and profitable for teaching, for reproof, for correction, for training in righteousness; that the man of God may be adequate, equipped for every good work" (2 Tim. 3:15-17, *NASB*).

The word of God in the larger sense portrayed *in* the Bible is therefore available to every person *through* the Bible, the *written* Word of God. All may hear the living Word by coming to the Bible humbly, persistently, with burning desire to find God and live in peace with Him.

As for others, the Bible may prove a deadly snare as it

did for those in Christ's earthly days who actually used the Bible to dismiss His person and His claims on them (John 5:36-47). Because of this we are warned *in* the Bible that we can destroy ourselves by Bible study: specifically, by the study of Paul's epistles, "in which are some things hard to understand, which the untaught and unstable distort, as they do also the rest of the Scriptures, to their own destruction" (2 Pet. 3:16, *NASB*).

Our only protection from our own pride and fear and ignorance and impatience as we study the Bible is the living Word, the Lord Himself, invoked in constant supplication.

O send Thy Spirit, Lord, now unto me,
That He may touch my eyes, and make me see;
Show me the truth concealed within Thy word,
And in Thy book revealed, I see the Lord.
(Mary Ann Lathbury)[10]

Light up Thy word; the fettered page
From killing bondage free:
Light up our way; lead forth this age
In Love's large liberty.

O Light of light! Within us dwell,
Through us Thy radiance pour,
That word and life Thy truths may tell,
And praise Thee evermore.
(Washington Gladden)[11]

Questions

1. "A kingdom is the type of thing that is controlled by a special kind of force—the power of a word." Discuss.

2. What is the lesson to be learned from the story of Jesus and the centurion?

3. What are the external and internal expressions of God's mind?

4. Why are the words of some persons more powerful than the words of others?

5. Some students of the New Testament have been troubled by how rarely Jesus ever prayed for a need brought before Him. What did Jesus typically do instead? Is there any lesson here for us?

6. How does a life in which one speaks the creative word of God differ from superstition, magic and voodoo? Can you recognize any tendencies toward superstition in a church or religious group known to you?

7. What is the *primary* meaning of "word of God"? What is the Bible's relation to that meaning?

8. What do legalism and superstition have in common?

Notes

1. Plato, *Theaetetus,* p. 190 of the Stephanus edition.
2. St. Augustine, *On the Trinity,* book 4, Ch. 10.
3. William Penn, *The Peace of Europe, Etc.* (London: J.M. Dent, n.d.), p. 65.
4. Mary W. Calkins, ed., *Berkeley: Essay, Principles and Dialogues with Selections from Other Writings* (New York: Charles Scribner's Sons, 1929), p. 370.
5. Ibid., p. 373.
6. Dylan Thomas, "The Hand That Signed the Paper Felled a City." *The Golden Treasury* (New York: New American Library), p. 455.
7. *Spurgeon's Lectures to His Students,* edited by David Otis Fuller (Grand Rapids: Zondervan Publishing House, 1945), p. 182.
8. Consider on this point the studies of the physiologist Walter Cannon, referred to in *Psychology Today,* June, 1983, pp. 71-72.
9. Mary Ann Lathbury, "Break Thou the Bread of Life," v. 1.
10. Ibid., v. 3.
11. Washington Gladden, "The Holy Scriptures."

CHAPTER 7

REDEMPTION THROUGH THE WORD OF GOD

It is too small a thing that You should be My Servant to raise up the tribes of Jacob, and to restore the [survivors] of Israel; I will also make You a light of the nations so that My salvation may reach to the end of the earth. (Isaiah 49:6, NASB*).*

You are the light of the world (Matthew 5:14, NASB*).*

To understand guidance we must in some good measure understand what the Word of God is. For in The Way of Christ guidance is essentially one dimension of a kind of life as a whole—of *eternal* life—a life lived in conversational relationship with God. Our studies of the Word of God are then necessary that we might better understand what the eternal kind of life is and how we are by the graciousness of God, to take part in it. Lack of understanding of and confidence in the Word of God as a substantial reality flatly rules out the possibility of any great degree of competence and confidence in guidance itself.

But, to renew a theme we mentioned earlier, God's guidance *of* us is not something given only *for* us and our purposes. It is not for our prosperity, safety, or amusement. Those who receive the grace of God's saving companionship in the ambience of the Word are by that very fact also fitted to show mankind how to live, how *to be the light of the world.* Their transformed nature automatically suits them to this task which, therefore, is *not* something *optional* or tacked on externally as an afterthought. The light which they radiate is not what they *do* over and above what they *are.*

Individuals close at hand, as well as world events at large, demonstrate what great need there is for light on how to live. There is no disagreement about this; and the popular media of newspaper, radio, and television, as well as scholarly research and publications, constantly update our burgeoning social and personal problems. These problems remain unsolved because of confusion, ignorance, and perversity in our leaders and in most of the world's population with regard to the causes of human happiness and misery.

Solutions to the problems of humanity—from incest to atomic warfare, from mental illness to poverty—are by no means easy or simple. But what we know of human nature seems clearly to indicate that light on how to live can be brought forward in an effective manner only by those who are prepared to *lead the way.* Only by *showing* how to live can we teach how to live. It is by our example—more precisely, by the kind of life that is in us and makes us exemplary as a God-indwelt people—that we lay the basis for communication of divine word and Spirit to an even larger circle of human beings. This is the pattern set forth in the New Testament book of Acts. In us, as in Jesus Christ Himself, *the life* is to be *the light* of men (John 1:4).

Collectively, the called-out people of God, the Church, is empowered to stand forth to wandering humanity like the cloudy pillar by day and the pillar of fire by night which guided the Israelites through the desert (Exod. 13). When faced with starvation, crime, economic disasters and difficulties, disease, loneliness, alienation, and war, the Church should be, it *could* be, the redeemed community to which the world looks for answers; for that community has the resources of God's government at its disposal. However dimly, we sense this and say this when we say, "Christ is the answer."

Individually, the disciple and friend of Jesus who has learned to work shoulder to shoulder with his or her Lord stands in this world as a point of contact between heaven and earth, a kind of Jacob's ladder by which the angels of God ascend from and descend into human life (John 1:51; Gen. 28:12). Thus the disciple stands as an envoy and transmitter by which the Kingdom of God is itself conveyed into every quarter of human affairs (Luke 10:1-11). This, as Hannah Hurnard has so beautifully described it, is the role of the intercessor:

> An intercessor means one who is in such vital contact with God and with his fellow men that he is like a live wire closing the gap between the saving power of God and the sinful men who have been cut off from that power. An intercessor is the contacting link between the source of power (the life of the Lord Jesus Christ) and the objects needing that power and life.[1]

But what is *the process* by which we can be transformed into children of Light—"blameless and innocent, children of God above reproach in the midst of a crooked and perverse generation, among whom you appear as lights in the world, holding fast the word of life" (Phil. 2:15-16, *NASB*)? How are we to understand the process of redemption, of being shaped and conformed to the likeness of the Son (Rom. 8:29)? This is the question to be dealt with in this chapter. When it is answered we shall at last be in position to deal specifically and fully with divine guidance in The Way of Christ.

An Additional Birth by the Word of God

"Let this mind be in you, which was also in Christ Jesus" (Phil. 2:5).

"For you have been called . . . to follow in His steps, who committed no sin, nor was any deceit found in His mouth; and while being reviled, He did not revile in return; while suffering, He uttered no threats, but kept entrusting Himself to Him who judges righteously" (1 Pet. 2:21-23, *NASB*).

In the light of our previous chapter on the word of God we can give a clear and thorough answer to the question about the process of redemption, and one which goes beyond mere figures of speech and poetic language. *It is through the action of the word of God upon us, through us, and with us that we come to have the mind of Christ and thus to live fully in the Kingdom of God.*

We now hold clearly before our minds what we have learned about the word of God: that it is a creative and sustaining substance, an active power, not limited by space and time and physical constraints, organizing and guiding that upon which it is directed by God and by man-with-God.

Life, in its various levels and types, is *power to act and respond in specific kinds of relations.* A cabbage has certain powers of action and response and a corresponding level of life. There is a difference between a cabbage that is alive and one that is dead, though the dead one still exists. Similarly for a snail or a kitten. But as the live cabbage (as well as the dead) has no response to a ball of string and is, though alive as a cabbage, *dead to* the realm of play, so a kitten playing with the string has no response to numbers and is dead to the realm of arithmetic. The live cabbage, though dead to one realm, is yet alive in another—that of the soil and the sun and the rain. Similarly with the kitten.

Man was once alive to God. He was created to be responsive to and interactive with Him. Adam and Eve lived in a conversational relationship with their Creator, daily renewed. When they mistrusted God and disobeyed, they were cut off from the realm of the Spirit and were dead in relation to it much as the kitten is dead to arithmetic. As God had said, "In the day that thou eatest thereof thou shalt surely die" (Gen. 2:17). Biologically they continued to live, of course, but they ceased to be responsive and interactive in relation to God's kingly cosmic rule. It would be necessary that God confer a new level of life upon them and their children in order for them to live unto God, be able to respond toward and act within the realm of the Spirit.

Man born of water (John 3:5)—that is, of semen and of the fluid in the sack which bursts as he exists in the womb—is alive in "the flesh," in the biological and psychosocial realm of nature. But he remains "dead in trespasses and sins" (Eph. 2:1) in relation to God, therefore "having no hope and without God in the world" (Eph. 2:12). He can have, however, be born a second time, born "from above" (John 3:3, *JB*)—which is not "born again" in the sense that a birth is *repeated,* a new start from the same place. He can have, instead, an *additional* birth whereby he becomes aware of and enters into the spiritual Kingdom of God. This additional bit is one brought about by the Spirit and is spiritual in its effects. "That which is born of the flesh is flesh; and that which is born of the Spirit is spirit" (John 3:6).

A respected "spiritual" leader of the Jews was very impressed with what he had seen of Jesus, and approached Him with the words: "Rabbi, we know that you are a teacher come from God; for no one can do these signs that you do, unless God is with him" (John 3:2, *RSV*). Thus he complimented Jesus, and he complimented himself on being an insider who had the good sense to recognize God at work.

Jesus' reply to him was a stinging rebuke. In effect He told him he had not the slightest idea of what he was talking about. Nicodemus was claiming to be able to recognize, to "see" God at work. Jesus said: "Unless a man is born from above, he cannot see the kingdom of God" (v. 3, *JB*), he cannot recognize God's workings. This immediately tripped up Nicodemus, revealed the level of his understanding, for he could only think of the fleshly birth; and he asked: "How can a grown man have *that* again?" Then Jesus explained that unless one has had *that* birth "of water" and an additional birth of Spirit he cannot *enter into* God's governance, His "Kingdom."

Those born of the Spirit manifest a life, a range of activities and responses, coming from an invisible power. In natural terms one cannot explain what is happening in them, "Where they come from, or where they go" (v. 8). But just as with the wind, we know the presence of God's Kingdom in a person by its effects.

We have already seen that the words of Jesus are spirit, and in what sense the spirit is also a word. Now we find that the *additional* birth which brings one to life in the realm of God is attributed both to *the Spirit* (John 3:5-8) and to *the word.*

In 1 Peter 1:23 those who are alive to God are described as being "born again not of seed which is perishable, but imperishable, that is, through the living and abiding word of God" *(NASB)*. And James 1:18 tells us that "of his own will begat he us with the word of truth."

The testimony of James and Peter was based on their *observation* of the effects which the words of God through Christ had had on them and of the effects which God's words through them and the early Church had had on others. It was a sober matter of fact which Paul expressed: "Faith is awakened by the message, and the message that awakens it comes through the word of Christ" (Rom. 10:17, *NEB*).

As the word of God in creation brought forth light and matter and life, so the gospel of Christ comes to man biologically alive but dead to God. It calls forth a response by its own power, enabling man to see and enter the Kingdom of God. Redemption in this respect is but a further aspect of creation, a "new creation." This new creation is the only thing that matters in man's relation to God, as Paul says (Gal. 6:15). Without it there is no relation to God in which man lives, and from it there arise all further developments of God's rule in the soul of man.

We quote once again from Spurgeon:

> Even so we have *felt* the Spirit of God operating upon our hearts, we have known and perceived the power which He wields over human spirits, and we know Him by frequent, conscious, personal contact. By the sensitiveness of our spirit we are as much made conscious of the presence of the Spirit of God as we are made cognizant of the existence of souls, or as we are certified of the existence of matter by its action upon our senses. We have been raised from the dull sphere of mere mind and matter into the heavenly radiance of the spirit-world; and now, as spiritual men, we discern spiritual things, we feel the forces which are paramount in the spirit-realm, and we know that there is a Holy Ghost, for we feel Him operating upon our spirits.[2]

The Engrafted Word of God

A figure which is used by James, the Lord's brother, to portray the relationship of the additional life of the Spirit to our natural, fleshly life is that of a *graft.* Graft is now more commonly understood as a kind of political corruption where someone taps into the flow of public wealth to enrich themselves. This, however, is but a figure of speech drawn from the original usage of the term, where "grafting" is a horticultural practice commonly done with various kinds of fruit trees and plants.

If you go to a plant nursery in the spring you will find small fruit trees ready to be planted in the yard or orchard. Very often they will bear tags which say things like "Santa Rosa Plum on Namgard" or "Elberta on Wild Peach." If you look toward the base of the tree you will discover a swelling which encompasses the trunk and looks as if the trunk has been broken and had healed itself. Now this is where the top of a little sapling with a vigorous root—usually some wild variety of the same genetic type—has been cut off, and a branch from a more desirable variety of fruit tree carefully attached so that the life of the more vigorous root will flow into the new branch. The superior energies of the wild and useless root are transformed, by passing through the substance of the imposed branch, to produce delicious and abundant fruit foreign in nature to its source in the root.

This practice of the orchard keeper was familiar to the writers of Scripture. Paul uses it to explain the relationship of the Gentiles to the Jewish nation (Rom. 11:17) in order that the Gentile Church might understand its dependence upon the Jews. James, after indicating that we are *begotten* with the word of truth, admonishes those who therefore have the additional life to "do away with all the impurities and bad habits that are still left in you, and humbly receive the engrafted word, which is able to save your souls" (see Jas. 1:21).

This figure signifies that, after the coming of our "additional" life, our natural powers are not merely left to run their own way under or alongside the new life, but are to be channeled through and subordinated to that life. All is redirected to spiritual ends, appointed to higher purposes, though they remain in themselves normal human powers.

The uniqueness of each individual personality is preserved in the beauty and goodness of its natural life, but a holy radiance rests upon and throughout it because it is now the temple of God, the area over which the larger and higher power of God plays.

Washed in the Word of God

We have seen how an additional and spiritual life comes through the word of God, and how that word then redirects the energies of the natural life to promote the ends of God's Kingdom. A further function of the word of God in our redemption is seen in Ephesians 5:25-27. Here, speaking of the Church, the apostle says that Christ "gave himself for it; that he might sanctify and cleanse it with the washing of water by the word, that he might present it to himself a glorious church, not having spot, or wrinkle, or any such thing; but that it should be holy and without blemish."

Here the word is pictured as washing away the impurities and clutter which permeate human personality, and which therefore afflict and hinder the role of Christ's corporate followers as the light of the world.

By His sacrificial death and triumphant resurrection, Jesus Christ welded His immediate followers into a totally new kind of social unit—the redemptive community, the living temple of the living God (Eph. 2:21-22). This in turn provided an environment within which God's word could be present with such richness and power that the church *could* stand forth on the world scene as beyond all reasonable reproach, and thus fulfill the calling to be the light of the world, the haven and guide of all mankind upon the earth.

Think for a moment what happens when we wash a shirt that is dirty. The water and cleansing agent *moves through* the fibers of the shirt and carries out the dirt lodged within them. Our minds and hearts are like the dirty shirt, cluttered with false beliefs and attitudes, with misguided plans and hopes and fears. The word of God—primarily the gospel of His Kingdom and of the life and death of Jesus on our behalf—enters our mind and brings new life through faith. As we open our entire lives to this new power and as those appointed by God to minister the word to us do their work, the word moves into every part of our personality, just like the water in the fibers of the shirt, to push out and replace all that is false and opposed to God's purposes in creating us and placing us where we are.

We are transformed by the renewing of our mind, and thus are "able to discern the will of God, and to know what is good, acceptable, and perfect" (Rom. 12:2, *NEB*). The mind thus transformed is the one for which divine guidance becomes a completely obvious and practical matter.

What a multitude of things must be washed from the mind! And only the powerful, living word of God is capable of this task. For example, we think that if we are mean enough to people they will be good. We hope to control people by punishing them. And yet this was not the way of Jesus. He let others punish Him, and said, "And I, if I be lifted up from the earth [on the cross], will draw all men unto me" (John 12:32). We believe that we must serve ourselves or no one else will. But He knew that anyone who would save his life must lose it (Luke 9:24-25). We are convinced that we gain by grabbing, but He taught us to "give, and it shall be given unto you" (Luke 6:38). An untold number of other false ideas and attitudes corrupt our minds and must be washed out by the entry of His word. "The entrance of thy words giveth light" (Ps. 119:130).

Even for those who already profess to follow Christ, much inward change may yet be needed. When trouble comes, when we have car trouble or get crosswise of someone in our family or at work, how long does it take us to get around to bringing it to God in prayer? When we observe an auto accident or violence, or hear an ambulance careening down the street, do we *think* to hold those concerned up to God in prayer? When we go to meet with a person for any reason, do we go in a spirit of prayer that we would be prepared to minister to them in all ways possible? When we are alone, do we constantly recognize that God is present with us? Does our mind spontaneously return to God when not intensely occupied, as the needle of the compass turns to the North Pole when removed from nearer magnetic sources? These questions make us sadly aware of how our mind is trained in false ways.

Today with all our knowledge, with all our technology and our sophisticated research, we are in the same situation as those who were described by Isaiah many centuries before Christ: "We hope for light, but behold, darkness; for brightness, but we walk in gloom. We grope along the wall like blind men, we grope like those who have no eyes; we stumble at midday as in the twilight *(NASB),* like dead men in the ghostly underworld" (*NEB,* Isa. 59:9-10), all because our brains, our minds, need to have the false thoughts washed out of them. They so badly need to be washed that we rarely understand what life would be like if they were cleaned.

A recent report from a mental health clinic told how the removal of coffee from the waiting rooms transformed the patients' behavior. Before, while the coffee was available, there was constant bickering and even violence between the patients as well as between the patients and the staff. After coffee was removed and the stimulation of caffeine withdrawn, there were only two or three unpleasant scenes per week. Like the caffeine, the poisonous thoughts, beliefs, fears, lusts, and attitudes which inhabit our minds compel human beings to destructive behavior with they themselves do not understand and whose source they do not recognize.

We recall what a word is: a word is fundamentally a thought expressed. The *literal* truth is that Christ removes the old routines in the mind, the old routines of thought and feeling and action and imagination, concepts, beliefs, inferences, and in their place puts something else—His thoughts, His words. He washes out the mind, and in the place of hatred, suspicion, and fear—to speak of emotions—he places love, confidence, and hopefulness.

So, where there was fear there is now hope; where there was suspicion there is now confidence; where there was hate there is now love; and all based upon a new understanding of God. Vessels of wrath become vessels of patience and kindness. Where there was covetousness and lust there is now generosity and consideration. Where there was manipulation and possessiveness there is now trust toward God and encouragement toward liberty and individuality.

Like the wild Gadarene (Mark 5), the legion of torments is gone, and now in life we sit with Jesus, "clothed, and in [our] right mind" (v. 15).

Union with Christ

We have been thus far dealing with the word of God as it comes to, upon, and throughout us. But in the progress of God's redemptive work *communication* advances into *communion,* and communion into *union.* When the progression is complete we can truly say: "Not I, but Christ liveth in me" (Gal. 2:20), and "For to me to live is Christ" (Phil. 1:21).

In communication there is a certain distance, even a possible opposition. We can communicate even with those with whom we are at war. God communicates with us even while we are His enemies, dead in trespasses and sins. When communication becomes communion, there is still distinctness, but also a profound *sharing* of thought and feeling and objectives that make up our lives. Each recognizes the thought or feeling as his or hers, but knows the other to be feeling or thinking in the same way. When communion advances into union, however, the sense of mine and thine may often be absent. There is only an "ours," and while "mine" does mean mine it no longer thereby means "not thine." This condition of union is realized in a marriage that indeed is one; and it is for this reason that marriage can serve as a picture of the relation between Christ and His church, and between the soul and its God.

It is this union beyond communion which Paul speaks of in describing the redeemed as having the mind of Christ (1 Cor. 2:16), as well as in exhorting us to have the mind of Christ (Phil. 2:5). It is this same union which Jesus prays for among the faithful "that they may be one, just as We are one; I in them, and Thou in Me, that they may be perfected in unity, that the world may know that Thou didst send Me, and didst love them, even as Thou didst love Me!" (John 17:22-23, *NASB*).

We must begin to appreciate the literal character of the Scriptures which speak of Christ being *in* us. Jesus Christ imparts *Himself* to His Church. In what may have been His first attempt to make this plain, He told His followers: "Truly, truly, I say to you, unless you eat the flesh of the Son of Man and drink His blood, you have no life in yourselves. He who eats My flesh and drinks My blood has eternal life; and I will raise him up on the last day. For My flesh is true food, and My blood is true drink" (John 6:53-55, *NASB*). Those who heard these words took deep offense, for they did not understand that when He spoke of His flesh and blood He was speaking in the most concrete terms of Himself. As He immediately explained, His literal flesh, when taken apart from the spiritual, the personal, would do them no good (v. 63). It is in this same verse that He describes His *words* as spirit and as life.

It was through His *words* that He imparted *Himself* as He lived and taught among the Jews of His day. And, upon the foundation of His words to His followers, the powerful events of Calvary, the resurrection presence, and Pentecost brought forth a communion and then a union later expressed by the Apostle Paul as "Christ in you, the hope of glory" (Col. 1:27).

Christ's Faith as My Faith

The faith by which Jesus Christ lived, His faith in God and His Kingdom, is expressed in the gospel which He Himself preached. That gospel is the good news that the kingdom rule of God is available to mankind here and now. His followers did not have this faith within themselves, and long regarded it only as *His* faith. Even after they came to have faith *in Him,* they did not share His faith.

Once in the midst of the Sea of Galilee, their boat was almost beaten under by the waves while Jesus slept calmly. His disciples awoke Him crying, "Lord save us: we perish" (Matt. 8:25)! He said, "Why are you such cowards? . . . How little faith you have!" (v. 26, *NEB*).

Now they obviously had great faith *in Him.* They called upon Him, counting on Him to save them. They had great faith in Him, but they did not have *His great faith in God,* and it was because they did not have *His* faith that He spoke of how little faith they had.

The contrast and relationship between having faith *in* Christ and having the faith *of* Christ is brought out, I believe, by the wording of Galatians 2:16,20, as this passage is translated in the King James version: "Knowing that a man is not justified by the works of the law, but by the faith *of* Jesus Christ, even we have believed *in* Jesus Christ that we might be justified by the faith *of* Christ, and not by the works of the law" (v. 16, italics added). Further discussion of the relation of the works of the law to the believer culminates in the great declaration of union, of identification, with Christ: "I am crucified with Christ: nevertheless I live; yet not I, but Christ liveth in me: and the life which I now live in the flesh I live by the faith *of* the Son of God, who loved me, and gave himself for me" (v. 20).

My suggestion is that Paul here presents faith *in* Christ—such as the apostles certainly had in the incident of the storm at sea—as that which leads to having the faith *of* Christ. It leads to the believer actually having the same faith in God that Jesus Himself had. Most modern translations, it is to be admitted, translate the *of's* from the above passages as *in's*. Thus the *New American Standard Bible:* "Knowing that a man is not justified by the works of the Law but through faith *in* Christ Jesus, even we have believed in Christ Jesus, that we may be justified by faith in Christ, and not by the works of the Law" (v. 16, italics added). And likewise: "The life which I now live in the flesh I live by faith *in* the Son of God" (v. 20, italics added).

In this reading the work of redemption and the power of the new life is brought by my faith in the person of Christ. But in the reading which the older translation gives, by contrast, it is Christ's faith *within* me that is my life, my redemption from the power of sin and darkness.

A similar point is to be made with reference to 2 Corinthians 5:14. Here Paul is attempting to explain his behavior as an "ambassador for Christ" (v. 20), and in so doing remarks: "The love of Christ (agape Christo) constrains us (v. 14). Or as the *New American Standard* says: "The love of Christ controls us." Not mere love *for* Christ, which is in me and directed toward Him; but the love *of* Christ, which is in me—mine *and yet* His in the union of our lives—and directed toward God the world of people for whom He lived and died and lives.

Now I do indeed understand that the grammatical forms involved here can be read as the "objective genitive," permitting the translation of these passages *without* the sense of "of" which I am suggesting. But on the other hand they do not *require* this reading, omitting the "of" and replacing it by "in" or "for." It is, however, the view of the new life which Paul and John the apostle teach as a life in union with Christ which forces us to take the "of" seriously, and not degrade it into a mere "in" or "for."

Faith in Christ and love for Christ leave Christ *outside*

the personality, and can never yield a "not I, but Christ liveth in me!" It can never provide the unity of the branches with the vine where the life that is in the branch is literally that which flowed through the Vine to which it attaches (John 15:1-4). It cannot provide that mutual "abiding in" (John 15:5) which causes us branches to bring forth much fruit and without which we can do nothing (v. 5). It is thus that we "were reconciled to God through the death of His Son, much more, having been reconciled, we shall be *saved by His life*" (Rom. 5:10, *NASB*, italics added).

Our "additional" life, though it is *our* life, is also Him living in us: His thoughts, His faith, His love, literally imparted to us by His word.

The teachings of Paul about salvation are hopelessly distorted when we fail to take literally his words about union and identification with Christ. His writings may be subjected to elaborate "plans of salvation," or the "Roman Road" of doctrinal assents by which we supposedly gain God's approval *merely* for believing what every devil in and out of hell believes to be true about Jesus and His work.

James S. Stewart's book *A Man in Christ,* deals with this tendency in interpreting Paul, and forcefully corrects it:

> Beyond the reproduction in the believer's spiritual life of his Lord's death and burial lies the glorious fact of *union with Christ in His resurrection.* "Like as Christ was raised up from the dead by the glory of the Father, even so we also should walk in newness of life." (Rom. 6:4) Everything that Paul associates with salvation—joy, and peace, and power, and progress, and moral victory—is gathered up in the one word he uses so constantly, "life." Only those who through Christ have entered into a vital relationship to God are really "alive." . . .

> But what Paul now saw with piercing clearness was that this life into possession of which souls entered by conversion was *nothing else than the life of Christ Himself.* He shared His very being with them.[3]

Stewart points out how Paul speaks of "Christ, who is our life" (Col. 3:4) and of "the life of Jesus" being "made manifest in our body" (2 Cor. 4:10). He points to Paul's contrast of "the law of sin and death" with "the law of the Spirit" which "brings the life which is in Christ Jesus" (Rom. 8:2); and he emphasizes, as we also have above, that "this life which flows from Christ into man is something totally different from anything experienced on the merely natural plane. It is different, not only in degree, but also in kind. It is *kainotes zōās* (Rom. 6:4), a new quality of life, a supernatural quality."[4] This is what is meant by Paul when he says that if anyone is *in* Christ he is a new creation (2 Cor. 5:17).

It is this identity between the "additional" life of the regenerate and the person and life of Christ Himself which turns the believers into "a colony of heaven" (as Moffatt translates Phil. 3:20), and enables them to fulfill the function of being the light of the world, showing the world how to live.

Reckon, Acknowledge Your Aliveness to God

The person who has been brought into the additional life by the creative action of the word of God now lives between two distinct realms of life and power: that of the natural or fleshly, and that of the supernatural or spiritual. Even while dead in trespasses and sin and unable to interact with God, one is capable of sensing the vacuum in the natural life apart from God and of following up on the many earthly rumors about God and where He is to be found. Once the new life begins to enter the soul, however, we then have the responsibility and opportunity of ever more fully focusing our whole being upon it, and wholly orienting ourselves toward it. This is *our* part, and God will not do it for us.

We see this happening in Romans 7. Here Paul speaks of a time when he found the impulses of his personality solidified through lifelong training in the ways of sin, continuing to move in their old patterns and not in conformity with the new life which entered his soul when he encountered Christ. In this condition, "I fail to carry out the things I want to do, and I find myself doing the very things I hate" (v. 15, *JB*).

It is like a boat traveling in the water. The boat does not immediately shift to the direction the pilot wants at the very moment he moves the rudder; and it may even continue moving forward for some time while the engine is in full reverse. The pilot must learn how to direct the ship or boat in terms of powers which, in some measure, move independently of his will and do not as such represent *his* intentions.

Paul *chooses* to identify with his new life; he *acknowledges, reckons, affirms* his union with that in him which cleaves to the good: "When I act against my own will, that means I have a self that acknowledges that the Law is good, and so the thing behaving in that way is not my self but sin living in me. The fact is, I know of nothing good living in me—living, that is, in my unspiritual self—for though the will to do what is good is in me, the performance is not, with the result that instead of doing the good things I want to do, I carry out the sinful things I do not want. When I act against my will, then, it is not my true self doing it, but sin which lives in me" (Rom. 7:16-20, *JB*). Or as the King James version simply says: "It is no more I that do it, but sin that dwelleth in me" (v. 20).

The "not I but sin" of this passage must be taken in conjunction with the "not I, but Christ" of Galatians 2:20. Of course a person might say such things and only be seeking to excuse themselves from responsibility for sin as in the case of Romans 7, or responsibility for action as in the case of Galatians 2. But not Paul. Paul—and he speaks for the hosts of men and women who have come to life in Christ throughout the ages—is beyond the point of excusing or accusing. He has accepted the full measure of his guilt before God and man. He is now concerned with how to enter into the new life to its fullest. This requires that *we* take a stand in the new energy from on high as to *who we are;* that *we* identify *with* the Christ life in us and *against* the sin still present in our members; that we settle in our will the question of who we *intend* to be.

This is what it means to *reckon* ourselves "to be dead indeed unto sin, but alive unto God through Jesus Christ our Lord" (Rom. 6:11).

As men and women of the additional birth, we stand at the intersection of the merely natural (fleshly) and the spiritual. Saint Thomas Aquinas coined a word to express just this state: *aevum,* as distinct from *tempus* and *aeternitas. Aevum* is the mean between eternity and time, sharing in them both. It is two lives, two streams of awareness and power, mingling together in the individual who must choose which *will be* him or her. Their identification with the one life or the other is not a *fact* to be *discovered* by subtle examinations of theological treatises or of their soul-life and states of mind. It is a set of the will: *will you* be the motions of sin in your members? Or *will you* be the resurrection life of Christ which has entered into you through the impact of God's word?

If we choose the latter, it is still with "fear and trembling" that *we work out* our own salvation, knowing that it is God Himself who is at work in us "both to will and to do of his good pleasure" (Phil. 2:12-13). It *is* I; yet it is *not I* but Christ. Beyond mere communication and communion we are in union with Him, and have the opportunity of progressively unifying all aspects of our personalities with Him so that truly "to me to live is Christ, and to die is gain" (Phil. 1:21).

The Written Word and the Progress of Redemption

Once the life of Christ has entered into us there are many things which we may do to increase the extent and depth of our identification and union with Him. But the proper use of the *written* word is central for our cooperative efforts with God toward our full conformity with Christ.

Of course the written word may come to us in many ways. It may come through sermon, through art, through casual conversation, through dramatic performance, literature, or song.

For many centuries, the contents of the Bible were present to the people of Europe through the architecture and artistry of their great cathedrals and churches. Indeed, even today, Christians who have read the Bible and know its contents well often are powerfully impacted upon first seeing the content of the Bible in magnificent stone and rich and sweeping stained-glass windows, such as in the cathedral at Chartres in France.

But while all of this is good and helpful, the one who wishes to grow in grace is by far best advised to make a close and constant companion of *the book,* the Bible. We do not mean that it should be worshiped. Its uniquely sacred character is something which does not need to be insisted upon, because it takes care of itself. But just as openness to and hunger for God leads naturally to the Bible, if it is available, so the Bible leads naturally to the mind of God and to the person of Christ.

The written word of God is an expression of God's mind—as surely, though in a different manner, as are creation and the living Word, Jesus. As we read and study it intelligently, humbly, and openly, we come evermore to share God's mind.

This use of the Bible is not superstitious or magical because there is a natural connection between a proper use of the Bible and its ideal result, union with Christ. It expresses the mind of God, since through its pages God Himself speaks to us. Thus we in understanding the Bible come to *share* His thoughts and attitudes, even are quickened by the Word to have His life. The Scripture is a *communication* which establishes *communion* and opens the way to *union,* all in a perfectly sensible manner once we begin to have the experience of it.

We will be spiritually safe in our use of the Bible if we follow a simple rule: *Read in a repentant attitude.* That is, read with readiness to surrender all we are, all of our plans, opinions, possessions, positions. Study as intelligently as possible, with all available means; but never *merely* to find the truth, and still less merely to prove anything. Subordinate your desire to find the truth to your desire to *do* it.

Those who wish to hear the word and know the truth often are not prompted by their desire to *do it.* The light which such people find is only their snare and condemnation.

Praying the Scriptures

"Therefore the Scriptures should only be read in an attitude of prayer, trusting to the inward working of the Holy Spirit to make their truths a living reality within us" (William Law).

There is a simple technique or routine which every believer, no matter how learned or how simple, can follow with assurance that the very bread of life will be spread for them upon the pages of the Scriptures. It is a practice very similar to one encouraged by Madame Guyon in her little book *Short and Very Easy Way of Prayer,* first published in 1688 in Lyons, France. It has been recently republished with some modifications under the title *Experiencing the Depths of Jesus Christ* (Christian Books, Goleta, CA, 1975). You will find it very useful to read the first four chapters of this little book as a supplement for what follows.

When we come to the Scriptures as a part of our conscious strategy to cooperate with God for our full redemption, we must *desire* that His will in all things revealed should be true for us. Next, we begin with those parts of the Scripture with which we have some *familiarity,* such as the Twenty-Third Psalm, the Lord's Prayer, the Sermon on the Mount, 1 Corinthians 13, or Romans 8.

Remember, first, your aim is not to become a scholar or to impress others with your knowledge of the Bible—quite a dreadful trap for so many biblical fellowships, which only cultivates pride and lays a foundation for the petty, quarrelsome spirit so commonly observed in students of the Scriptures. Your aim is to nourish your soul on God's Word to you. Hence, go to those parts you already know, and count on your later growth and study to lead you to other parts.

Secondly, do not try to read a great deal. As Madame Guyon wisely counsels: "If you read quickly, it will benefit you little. You will be like a bee that merely skims the surface of a flower. Instead, in this new way of reading with prayer, you must become as the bee who penetrates into the depths the flower. You plunge deeply within to remove its deepest nectar."[5]

You may have been told that it is good to read the Bible through every year, and that you can ensure this by reading so many verses per day from the Old and New Testaments. If you do this you may enjoy the reputation of one who reads the Bible through each year and you may compliment yourself upon it. But will you thereby become more like Christ and more filled with the life of God?

It is a proven fact that many who read the Bible in this way, like taking medicine or exercising on a schedule, do not advance spiritually. Better in one year to have ten good verses transferred into the substance of our lives than to have every word in the Bible flash before our eyes. Remember that "the letter killeth, but the spirit giveth life" (2 Cor. 3:6).

Now come to your chosen passage as to the place where you will meet God. Read a small part of the passage selected and dwell upon each of its parts, praying for the assistance of God's Spirit in bringing *fully* before your mind and into your life the realities expressed. Always ask: What is my life like since this is true, and how shall I speak and act because of this? You may wish to turn the passage into a prayer of praise or of request.

Perhaps you are reading the great "God is love" passage from 1 John 4. You find it here written, "There is no fear in love; but perfect love casts out fear, because fear involves punishment, and the one who fears is not perfected in love" (v. 18, *NASB*). You dwell upon the ways in which love from God to us and from us to Him and between people on earth pushes fear out. You think of the fearless child surrounded by loving parents, of how loving neighbors give us confidence and relax our fears. You dwell upon how assurance of God's love given to us in the death of His Son suggests that we will never get beyond His care. You then seek divine help in comprehending this and in realizing what your fear-free life might be like. Then lift your heart in joyful praise as you realize how things are for you in God's Kingdom. God's word speaking in you creates the faith which appropriates the fact *for you.*

Or read, "The Lord is my shepherd; I shall not want" (Ps. 23:1). First, there is *information* which we may not automatically transfer to ourselves. We may say: "This was true for David, the psalmist." But as we dwell prayerfully upon the mere information there arises a *yearning* that it might be so for *us*—"I wish the Lord were my shepherd; that the great God would have for me that care and attention which the shepherd has for his sheep!" And as we meditate upon the psalm *affirmation* may arise, as it has for so many people—"It must be so! I will have it to be so!" Then perhaps *invocation*—"Lord, make it so for me." Then *appropriation*—the settled conviction that it *is* so, a statement of fact for you.

Now practice the same type of process with those great passages from Romans 8—beginning with verse 28, for example, "All things work together for good to them that love God, to them who are the called according to his purpose," and culminating in the declaration of triumph that no matter what befalls us "we are more than conquerors through him that loved us" (v. 37). The general train of development again is *information, longing* for it to be so, *affirmation* that it *must* be so, *invocation* to God to make it so, and finally *appropriation* by God's grace of its being so. This last stage must not be forced or, especially, faked. The ability for it will be given.

When there is the inner agreement of our minds with the truth expressed in the passages, we have these parts of the mind of Christ in us as *our own*. For these great truths conveyed from Scripture were the very things which Jesus believed. They constituted faith and hope and love in which He lived. And as they become ours, His mind becomes our mind. We are outfitted then to function as true co-laborers with God, brothers and friends of Jesus in the Kingdom of God. And we are in position to know and understand in its fullness the *guidance* which God gives to His children.

Questions

1. "How are we to understand the process of redemption, of being shaped and conformed to the likeness of the Son?" What is the author's answer to this question? What is your opinion about the adequacy and practicality of that answer?

2. What is the definition of "life" given in this chapter? How can viewing your own life in terms of this definition help you grow in your Christian life?

3. "Grafting" and "washing" are two metaphors relating

to the "additional life" of the Christian. Explain the meaning of each in this context and illustrate each with practical applications.

4. "But in the progress of God's redemptive work *communication* advances into *communion*, and communion into *union*." Explain and illustrate.

5. What is the difference between (a) "the faith *of* Christ" and (b) "faith *in* Christ"?

6. What does it mean to "*reckon* ourselves to be dead unto sin"?

7. " . . . is not a *fact* to be *discovered* by subtle examinations of theological treatises or of their soul-life and states of mind. It is a set of the will . . . . " What is being discussed in this passage and what is the relevance of the point?

8. "We will be spiritually safe in our use of the Bible if we follow a simple rule . . . " What is that rule?

9. What is meant by "praying the Scriptures"? Have you tried it?

Notes

1. Hannah Hurnard, *God's Transmitters* (Wheaton, IL: Tyndale House Publishers, 1981), p. 12.

2. C.H. Spurgeon, *Lectures to His Students,* edited by David Otis Fuller (Grand Rapids: Zondervan Publishing House, 1945), p. 172.

3. James S. Stewart, *A Man in Christ* (London: Hodder and Stoughton, 1935), pp. 192-193.

4. Ibid., p. 193.

5. Madame Guyon, *Experiencing the Depth of Jesus Christ* (Goleta, CA: Christian Books, 1975), p. 16.

CHAPTER 8

KNOWING THE VOICE OF GOD

The shepherd in charge of the sheep . . . . calls his own sheep by name, and leads them out . . . . He goes ahead and the sheep follow, because they know his voice . . . . I am the good shepherd; I know my own sheep and my sheep know me . . . . My own sheep listen to my voice; I know them and they follow me (John 10:2-4,14,27, NEB*).*

The doctrine of the inner light is not sufficiently taught. To the individual believer, who is, by the very fact of relationship to Christ, indwelt by the Holy Spirit of God, there is granted the direct impression of the Spirit of God on the Spirit of man, imparting the knowledge of His will in matters of the smallest and greatest importance. This has to be sought and waited for (G. Campbell Morgan).[1]

When a word or thought comes to us—whether in our own thinking or by the inner voice, or some special experience, or from the Bible, or from circumstances—*how* do we know whether or not it is a word of God?

We can, of course, know that the word is from God if it is the plain statement and meaning of the Bible or if it can be obtained from biblical teaching as a whole by a sound manner of interpretation. But beyond this the only answer is *by experience.* And "beyond this" we certainly must go, for the general teachings of the Bible, no matter how thoroughly studied and firmly believed, can never by themselves constitute our personal walk with God. Moreover, a single statement taken directly from the Bible—and these so often are invoked for personal guidance—may be used contrary to the purposes of God. It is only the Bible as a whole that is *the* written Word of God.

Now it is a remarkable fact that sheep or other domesticated animals or pets quite unerringly recognize the voice of their master or mistress *by experience.* When they first hear the voice, they do not recognize who is speaking, but they very quickly learn to do so. They do not need a voice meter or other device to analyze it scientifically, but recognize it immediately, somewhat as we learn to recognize red, with its various shades and characteristics, and distinguish it from green or yellow, or as a musician recognizes a minor or major key simply by listening.

Comparison of man with animals on this point is a prophetic theme. Isaiah marvels that "an ox knows its owner, and a donkey its master's manger. But Israel does not know, my people do not understand" (1:3, *NASB*). Jeremiah renews the complaint with reference to nondomesticated creatures: "Even the stork in the sky knows her seasons; and the turtledove and the swift and the thrush observe the time of their migration. But my people do not know the ordinance of the Lord" (8:7, *NASB*).

The light that lighteth every human being that comes into the world (John 1:9) shines vainly into the blinded eyes of fallen humanity. The word which has gone out to the very ends of the earth (Ps. 19:4) falls upon deaf ears. Those who have been given the "additional" birth through the special redemptive message of Christ that has entered their lives *can,* however, *learn* to hear the speaking of God and confidently interact with it.

The simple statements quoted at the beginning of this chapter from the Gospel of John chapter ten are not merely a record of words which Jesus spoke, but are also an expression of John's own experience with Christ His Lord and friend. The emphasis given in the opening of his first Epistle to seeing, hearing, and touching the Word of Life (vv. 1,3) is quite startling, but it was in the presence of Jesus that John learned to recognize when *God* was speaking.

In the course of later experience he became so confident of the inner teacher that he could tell his children in the faith—precisely in a context where he was warning against those trying to deceive them—that they had no need of anyone other than the inner teacher, the Holy Spirit: "The anointing which you received from Him abides in you, and you have no need for any one to teach you; but as His anointing teaches you about all things, and is true and is not a lie, and just as it has taught you, you abide in Him" (1 John 2:27, *NASB*).[2]

John therefore speaks to us with the authority of experience, just as Abraham did to his eldest servant in sending him into an unknown land for Isaac's wife (Gen. 24), and just as Eli did to little Samuel (1 Sam. 3).

We may falsely suppose that if *God* spoke to us we would automatically know, without having to learn, *who* is speaking to us. But this is just a mistake, and one which I have come to regard as very dangerous in the search for guidance. Whether because of our fallen condition, or because of the very nature of all personal relations—you did not recognize the voice of the One now most dear and intimate to you the first time you heard it—or because of the gentleness of our Father who speaks, it seems we normally must be told *that* God is speaking to us and possibly be helped to detect His voice; and only later do we come without assistance to distinguish and recognize His voice as *His* voice.

Certainly it is true that the little child is first spoken to, and knows that it is being spoken to by a certain person, before it learns to recognize the voice itself as belonging to that person. And in general, as adults we can recognize a person's voice only after we are aware, by whatever means, that it is *they* who have spoken to us on a number of occasions.

With assistance from those who know about such things from their own experience, and with the right attitude on our part, we can come to know the voice of God without great difficulty. It is in the interest of *evil,* on the other hand, to make an inherent *mystery* of God's word to us, for then His direction of our lives is undermined. Without qualified assistance and the desire to learn and readiness to cooperate, however, the matter may never become clear, and guidance may remain a riddle to us, or at best a game of theological charades. This is generally the condition of the Church in the present day, I fear, and it explains why there is such great confusion and difficulty about divine guidance.

The Three Lights

"God's impressions within and his word without are always corroborated by his providence around, and we should quietly wait until those three focus into one point . . . . If you do not know what you ought to do, stand still until you do, And when the time comes for action, circumstances, like glowworms, will sparkle along your path; and you will become so sure that you are right, when God's three witnesses concur, that you could not be surer though an angel beckoned you on" (F.B. Meyer).[3]

If I could keep only one writing on divine guidance outside of the Bible itself, it would be hard to pass over a few pages from F.B. Meyer's book entitled *The Secret of Guidance.* Many other authors have very fine and helpful things to say on the subject, but Meyer draws the issues together in such a complete and yet simple fashion, and the spirit of his remarks—as is usual with him—is both so sane and so spiritual that he is certainly to be chosen over most who have written on this subject. According to Meyer:

> The circumstances of our daily life are to us an infallible indication of God's will, when they concur with the inward promptings of the spirit and with the Word of God. So long as they are stationary, wait. When you must act, they will open, and a way will be made through oceans and rivers, wastes and rocks.[4]

Now it is possible to understand this precious advice in such a way that it completely resolves any problem about divine guidance. I believe that this will normally be the case for those who have already learned to recognize the inner voice of God, and probably none knew it more clearly than Meyer himself. But for those who do not have a confident working familiarity with the Voice, the "three lights," as they are sometimes called,[5] may speedily become a swirl of confusion and leave us hopelessly adrift or wrecked upon the shoals of our spiritual misadventures. They can be especially dangerous and disappointing for those without a deep experience and commitment in The Way of Christ. For they will seek a spiritual gimmick to make sure of their own prosperity and security.

A large part of the problem in working with the "three lights" comes from their obvious *interdependence.*

First of all, it is commonly understood that the Scriptures depend upon the Holy Spirit for their efficacy in guidance as well as redemption. A recent conference of evangelical scholars affirms "that the Holy Spirit who inspired scripture acts through it today to work faith in its message," and "that the Holy Spirit enables believers to appropriate and apply scripture to their lives." It is likewise denied "that the natural man is able to discern spiritually the biblical message apart from the Holy Spirit."[6]

Many people commonly regarded as in the evangelical tradition seem prepared to make even stronger statements on the role of the Holy Spirit in Bible study. Consider again William Law:

> Without the present illumination of the Holy Spirit, the Word of God must remain a dead letter to every man, no matter how intelligent or well-educated he may be . . . . It is just as essential for the Holy Spirit to reveal the truth of Scripture to the reader today as it was necessary for Him to inspire the writers thereof in their day . . . . Therefore to say that because we now have all the writings of Scripture complete we no longer need the miraculous inspiration of the Spirit among men as in former days, is a degree of blindness as great as any that can be charged upon the scribes and Pharisees. Nor can we possibly escape their same errors; for in denying the present inspiration of the Holy Spirit, we have made Scripture the province of the letter-learned scribe.[7]

But how are we to recognize the intervention of the Holy Spirit—even in our studies of the Bible—except from the teachings of the Scriptures? The test of a spiritual impulse by its confession of Jesus as Lord (1 Cor. 12:3) or as Son of God (1 John 4:3) is not one which turns out to be practically helpful, in general, for those believers who are trying to decide whom to marry or which job to take. And testing of spiritual or mental impulses or messages cannot in general be done by invoking the teachings of Scripture, if Scripture in turn cannot be understood without spiritual assistance through those very impulses and "messages."

Finally, the mere "open" or "closed" doors of circumstances cannot function independently of the other two "lights," or of *some* additional factor; for one does not know merely by looking at these "doors" who is opening or closing them, God or Satan or human effort. Indeed, one often cannot tell whether they are "open" or "closed" until *after* one has acted. Hence one cannot use openness or closedness to determine what to do.

No doubt those who think they can make the "three lights" formula work will be very impatient with the difficulties here raised. My experience suggests that people who do not really need help in the practical context of guidance may think that this formula can be made to work *as* a formula—which is how it is normally presented. Those who do need help, on the other hand, frequently drive themselves to distraction trying to use it. Also, the formula is *in retrospect* often thought to have worked after one has taken a certain alternative at the suggestion of the "lights" and all has turned out well. But the confidence is here once again present precisely where it is no longer needed.

To repeat the problem: Circumstances mean one thing only if the Bible says such and such, and the Bible says such and such only if the Spirit directs our understanding. But we know that it was a spiritual impulse which suggested that the Bible says such and such only if the suggestion that it says such and such is in line with what the Bible says. And if the "door is open," then the Spirit *must* be leading, and hence we also *must* be following the Bible, for we are "succeeding." And if, on the other hand, the "door is closed," then we don't have to decide anyway, since the door is, precisely, closed. But *is* it closed, or does it just look that way? What does the Bible or Spirit say? And if it is closed and *we* can open it, *should* we open it? God helps those who help themselves! Such questions seem endless.

Thus it just is not true that one can get a reading of what circumstances "say," and a *separate* one of what the Bible says, and a further *separate* one of what the Spirit says. Consequently there is no way that we can strengthen our reading of God's will from one source by checking it against the other sources, as we well might get a safer reading of the time of day by consulting three clocks. In the matter concerned here, what we think the one "clock" says will often if not always depend on what we take the others to say.

And yet all who have much experience in The Way of Christ will know that it is *somehow* right to look for guidance in circumstances, the Bible, and inner impulses. And all will know that these three *somehow* serve to correct each other. While they provide *no formula* for making decisions, they must not be simply abandoned. How are we to understand the role they play in divine guidance?

The answer to this question comes in two parts. First of all, the life in which divine guidance is functioning is *not* one which excludes our own judgment. This is something we have already discussed, and we shall consider yet a new and very important aspect of it in our next and final chapter. The "three lights" are simply factors which we must consider in making a responsible judgment. Then secondly, while none of the "lights," nor all of them taken together, simply *give* us our guidance, each or all together may be and usually are the *occasion* of God's directive word coming to us. And this is the way in which, as a matter of fact, it usually works. The voice of God is not any one of the "three lights," nor all. But the inner anointing of which John speaks—or the voice or word of God coming to individuals as repeatedly displayed in biblical events—usually comes to us in conjunction with our study and meditation upon the Bible, with experiences of various kinds of "impressions" or feelings which we may have, or with contemplation of circumstances which befall us. Although there are exceptions to the rule, the divine directive does not usually come to us "out of the blue." This is important to us practically. It enables us to do specific, concrete things as we seek to know the will of God. These things we do—reflecting upon the three "lights"—turn out to be the very things which go into exercising responsible judgment. As we engage in them we also listen for the divine voice. But when we recognize the voice as *His* voice we do so because our experience enables us to recognize it, not because we are good at playing a guessing game about how the occasions through which it comes match up with each other.

Three Factors of Voice

"The voice of my beloved! behold, he cometh leaping upon the mountains, skipping upon the hills" (Song of Solomon 2:8).

"I sleep, but my heart waketh: it is the voice of my beloved" (Song of Solomon 5:2).

To say that we learn to recognize the voice of God by experience is not, however, all that we can say. There are certain factors which distinguish the voice of God, just as is the case in any human voice.

The most immediate factor in the human voice is one which is usually enough all by itself to tell those familiar with it whose voice it is: a certain *quality* of the sound produced. This is mainly a matter of which *tones* are produced and the manner in which they are modulated. "Quality" at the human level also includes the *style* of speech; for example, whether it is slow or fast, smooth or halting in its flow, indirect or to the point.

Besides quality, a certain *spirit* attaches to the human voice. A voice may be passionate or cold, whining or demanding, timid or confident, coaxing or commanding.

This of course is no mere matter of sounds but of attitudes which are tangibly present in the voice.

And then, finally, there is the matter of *content,* or of information conveyed. Although this is rarely the *immediate* sign of who is speaking, it is in the end the most conclusive mark, for it reveals the history and conscious experience of the speaker.

The three factors of quality, spirit, and content by no means exhaust the complexity of voice. Modern-day science and linguistics find in the voice vast fields of theoretical and practical study. From the philosophical point of view, there is yet much more to be said. Professor Don Ihde of the State University of New York has recently published a very helpful guide to a deeper examination of the phenomenon of voice in his *Listening and Voice.*[8] But enough has been said to allow us to turn to examination of the voice of God in our hearts.

The Weight of Authority

The question then is, What are the factors of *that* voice which enable us to recognize it as *God's* voice? Here too there is a distinctive quality with which we become familiar. But of course it is not the quality of a sound. Rather, its quality is more a matter of a certain weight of the impression which its communications make upon our consciousness. There is a certain steady and calm force with which it impacts our souls, eliciting assent and even conformity in action. The assent is frequently given or the conformity conceded before the content of the communication is fully grasped. We inwardly sense its immediate power; and once we have experienced it we do not any longer wonder at the biblical phenomena of nature and spirits responding to this divine word. The unquestionable authority with which Jesus spoke to nature, man, and demons was but a very clear manifestation of this quality of the word of God.

Addressing the question of how one can distinguish the

voice of God from one's own subconscious, E. Stanley Jones says,

> Perhaps the rough distinction is this: The voice of the subconscious argues with you, tries to convince you; but the inner voice of God does not argue, does not try to convince you. It just speaks and it is self-authenticating. It has the feel of the voice of God within it.[9]

When Jesus spoke, His words had a weight of authority which had the effect of opening up the understanding of the hearers and creating faith in them. "He taught them as one having authority, and not as the scribes" (Matt. 7:29). The authority of the scribe or mere scholar comes from his "footnotes," his references to someone other than himself who is supposed to know. The word of God, on the other hand, comes with a serene weight of authority *in itself*. People left the presence of Jesus with heads and hearts full of thoughts and convictions which He had authored in them through the power of God's voice or word that He spoke.

The immediate qualitative distinction of the voice of God is emphasized in John Wesley's first sermon on "The Witness of the Spirit." Here he poses the question, "But how may one who has the real witness in himself distinguish it from presumption?" He replies:

> How, I pray, do you distinguish day from night? How do you distinguish light from darkness; or the light of a star, or a glimmering taper, from the light of the noonday sun? Is there not an inherent, obvious, essential difference between the one and the other? And do you not immediately and directly perceive that difference, provided your senses are rightly disposed? In like manner, there is an inherent,

> essential difference between spiritual light and spiritual darkness; and between the light wherewith the Sun of righteousness shines upon our heart, and that glimmering light which arises only from "sparks of our own kindling": and this difference also is immediately and directly perceived if our spiritual senses are rightly disposed.
>
> To require a more minute and philosophical account of the manner whereby we distinguish these, and of the *criteria,* or intrinsic marks, whereby we know the voice of God, is to make a demand which can never be answered: no, not by one who has the deepest knowledge of God.[10]

In my own experience, I first became aware of God's word coming to me *by the effects* upon myself and others around me. The insights which came were often literally staggering. But as I became aware that it was *God's* word, I immediately began to observe the qualitative difference which Wesley so faithfully emphasizes, and to find that certain others understood exactly what it was. Adela Rogers St. John remarks, perhaps somewhat overconfidently, but yet to the point: "The first time you receive guidance you will know the difference. You can mistake rhinestones for diamonds, but you can never mistake a diamond for a rhinestone."[11]

The "Spirit" of God's Voice

The voice of God speaking in our souls also hears in it a characteristic *spirit.* It is a spirit of exalted peacefulness and confidence, or joy, of sweet reasonableness, and of will for the good. It is, in short, "the spirit of Jesus," and by that we refer to the overall tone of His personal life as a whole. Those who had seen Him had truly seen the Father who shared the same "Spirit." And it is this Spirit which marks the voice of God in our hearts. Any word which bears an opposite spirit most surely is not the voice of God.

Bob Mumford's statement about one of his experiences of guidance illustrates this point. The voice of God found him in Colombia, South America, and very distinctly said: "I want you to go back to school." His description of this experience brings out the quality and spirit of the voice:

> It couldn't have been any clearer if my wife had spoken the words right next to me. It was spoken straight and strong and right into my spirit. It wasn't a demanding, urgent voice. If it had been, I would immediately have suspected the source to be someone or something other than the Lord. The vocal impression was warm, but firm. I knew it was the Lord.[12]

The sweet spirit of God's voice carries over to the lives of those who speak with His voice: "The wisdom that is from above is first pure, then peaceable, gentle, and easy to be entreated, full of mercy and good fruits, without partiality, and without hypocrisy" (Jas. 3:17). Did we but heed this statement we would never lack for sure knowledge of who speaks for God and who does not.

Content

And then, finally, there is a *content* which marks the voice of God. Perhaps we had better speak of *a dimension* of the content, since the specific content of an individualized word from God may not of itself be easily identifiable as from God. But this much we can say: The content of a word which is truly from God will always conform to, be consistent with, the truths about God's nature and Kingdom that are made clear in the Bible, and any content or claim which does not conform to that content is not a word from God.

Evan Roberts, in college and studying for the ministry, was deeply moved by the sermons of Seth Joshua, who visited his college.

> Roberts could not concentrate on his studies after that and went to the principal of his college, and said, "I hear a voice that tells me I must go home and speak to the young people in my home church. Mr. Phillips, is that the voice of the devil or the voice of the Spirit?" Phillips answered, very wisely, "The devil never gives orders like that. You can have a week off."[13]

While this response may seem a little glib, it was basically right. Subsequent events showed that Roberts was indeed directed by the Lord.

The conformity which a thought or perception or other experience must have in order to qualify as the voice of God is conformity to the principles, the fundamental truths of Scripture. It is the *principles,* not the incidentals of Scripture, that count here. Study of the Scriptures makes clear that there are certain things that are fundamental, absolute, exceptionless; and they show up with stunning clarity as we become familiar with the overall content of Scripture.

Reading in 1 Corinthians 11, on the other hand, we find ladies advised not to have short hair, and men informed that long hair on them is shameful. Such things are incidentals. More seriously, in Mark 10 the fine young man who came to Jesus was to sell all that he had and give it to the poor. This too is an incidental except in the particular case, such as this young man, where it reached into the core of his particular problem. But it is not a principle to which all must conform. It is not a teaching emerging from the whole of Scripture, and should not without further considerations be taken as God's word to you. However, when you read John the apostle and learn from him "that God is light, and in him is no darkness" (1 John 1:5), you are on to a principle: something which wells up from the whole Bible and the totality of the experience of God's people.

When we hear Jesus saying, "The first of all the commandments is, Hear, O Israel; the Lord our God is one Lord: and thou shalt love the Lord thy God with all thy heart, and with all thy soul, and with all thy mind, and with all thy strength: this is the first commandment. And the second is like, namely this, Thou shalt love thy neighbor as thyself" (Mark 12:29-31), then we are in the presence of principles. When we hear it said that "Whosoever will save his life shall lose it; but whosoever shall lose his life for my sake and the gospel's, the same shall save it" (Mark 8:35), that too is a principle. When we hear it said, "Seek ye the kingdom of God; and all these things shall be added unto you" (Luke 12:31), that is a principle also. No specific guidance from God will ever contradict such principles.

Principles of Scripture are most of all to be identified from the actions, spirit, and explicit statements of Jesus Himself. When we take Him in His wholeness as our model and the one to follow, we will safely identify the content of the inner voice of God: "He that followeth me shall not walk in darkness, but shall have the light of life" (John 8:12). In the knowledge of this we are set free to let our experience be open to the new and special things which God wants to do in us and through us. We will be free to develop the power and authority that come from the experience of dealing directly with God—free *and* safe within the pattern of Christ's life.

Beware the Spiritual Panacea!

But something should also be said about content on the negative side. Any voice which promises total exemption from suffering and failure is most certainly *not* God's word. In recent years innumerable persons have offered ways of using the Bible and God as guarantees of health, success, and wealth. The Bible is treated as a "How-to" book, a manual for the successful life in the American way which, if followed, will assure you will prosper financially, that you will not get cancer or even a cold, and that your church will never split or lack a successful pastor and program. To the question from the old hymn:

> Shall I be carried to the skies,
>   On flowery beds of ease;
> While others fought to win the prize,
>   And sailed through bloody seas?[14]

these people shout, "Yes, most certainly!"

If we will but consider those who stand throughout history as the best practitioners of The Way, we will find that they went through great difficulties, often living their entire lives and dying amidst them. The word of God does not come just to lead us out of trouble—though that sometimes happens—or to make sure that we have it easy and that everything goes our way. And when we hear a suggestion that it does, we had better remember what Jesus said to Peter: "I'm going to go up to Jerusalem and they're going to kill me." And Peter—because he just *knew* it—said, "Far be it from thee, Lord. Such a thing shall not happen to thee." Peter did not have *that* in mind for himself, and hence not for his Messiah, the star to which he had hitched his wagon. But Jesus said to him, "Get thee behind me, Satan, for you have no liking for the things of God, but for the things of man" (see Matt. 16:21-23).

We must not be misled by wistful thinking. We are going to go through the mill of life like everyone else. We are different because we *also* have a higher or "additional" life, a different quality of life, a spiritual life, an eternal life, not because we are spared the ordinary troubles which befall ordinary human beings.

In summary, then, what we learn when we learn to

recognize God's voice in our heart is a certain *weight or force,* a certain *spirit,* and a certain *content.* These three things in combination mark the voice of God; and to the one well experienced in The Way of Christ they give great confidence and great accuracy in living as the friend of Christ and co-laborer with God in His Kingdom.

The Voice of Satan

It is in *contrast* with such a voice that we come also to know the voice of our adversary, Satan, when *he* speaks in our heart. Only if we recognize this voice can we avoid many silly attributions of events to Satan. And only so, also, can we implicitly *resist* him and make him flee from us. Satan will not come to us like an oversized bat with bony wings, hissing like a snake. And very seldom will he assume *any* external manifestation. He will come to us in our thoughts and our perceptions; and we must be alert to any *marked* contrast to the weight, spirit, and content of God's voice, for that may signify that we are under attack.

The temptations of Jesus in Matthew 4 illustrate this well. It does not take much imagination to realize that if some bat-like creature suggested to Jesus that He turn the stones into bread, this would certainly have tended to curb His appetite. How *did* "the tempter [come] to him" (v. 3)?

I would only suggest that as Jesus suffered extreme hunger the stones about Him reminded him of—began to *look* like—the loaves from his mother's oven. Perhaps He began to *smell* them, and then to think how easily he could turn those stones into such loaves—with butter!

But then he realized the *conflict* of this vision with the great truth that the word of God is a substance, a meat (John 4:32); and He refused to allow Himself to be turned away from learning the sufficiency of that word to His every need. Man lives by the word from God's mouth (Deut. 8:3). The voice of temptation was opposed in spirit and content to God's word, and Satan was recognized and successfully resisted both in this and in the other temptations which followed.

Every follower of Christ must be encouraged to believe that he can come to understand and distinguish the voice of God if he will but look within his mind for much the same *kinds* of distinctions within his thoughts and perceptions as he would find in the communications received from other human beings through spoken or written language: *a distinctive quality, spirit and content.* All of the guidance which we are going to receive from God, no matter what the external or internal accompaniments may be, will ultimately take the form of our own thoughts and perceptions. We must learn to find in them the voice of that God in whom we live and move and have our being.

Infallibility?

But, someone may say, When I am sure that God is speaking to me, and sure about what He says, *could I not still be mistaken,* even though I have much apparently successful experience at hearing and understanding His voice? The answer is yes, of course, you still *could* be wrong. God does not by His conversational walk with us intend to make us infallible. You also *could* be wrong about most of the beliefs upon which you very successfully base your life. But you are normally correct. You always *could* be wrong in believing that your gas gauge is working, that your bank is reliable, that your food is not poisoned. Such is human life, and our walk with the Lord does not exempt us from the possibility of error even in the reading of what His voice is saying. Infallibility, and especially infallibility in discerning the mind of God, simply does not become our humble condition, and should not be desired, much less expected, from our relationship with God.

The Centrality of the Bible

Personally, I somehow find comfort and encouragement in the face of my fallibility by close association with the Bible. We have repeatedly emphasized the centrality of the written Word in the functioning of divine guidance. It cannot be too much stressed that the permanent address at which the word of God may be contacted is the Bible. More of God's speaking to me, personally, has come in conjunction with study and teaching of the Bible than with anything else. As F.B. Meyer says, "The [written] Word is the wire along which the voice of God will certainly come to you if the heart is hushed and the attention fixed."[15] Reading in the lives of the saints seems to confirm this. From the many available illustrations we select a few words from John Bunyan:

> One day, as I was travelling into the country and musing on the wickedness and blasphemy of my heart, and considering the enmity that was in me to God, that scripture came into my mind: "Having made peace through the blood of His cross." (Col. 1:20). By which I was made to see, both again and again, that God and my soul were friends by his blood; yea, I saw that the justice of God and my sinful soul could embrace and kiss each other, through his blood. This was a good day to me; I hope I shall never forget it.
>
> At another time, as I sat by the fire in my house and was musing on my wretchedness, the Lord made that also a precious word unto me: "Forasmuch then as the children are partakers of flesh and blood, he also himself likewise took part of the same; that through death he might destroy him that had the power of death, that is, the devil; and deliver them who through fear of death were all their lifetime subject to bondage." (Heb. 2:14-15) I thought that the glory of these words was then so weighty on me, that I was both once and twice ready to swoon as I sat, yet not with grief and trouble, but with solid joy and peace.[16]

It is by experience that many in addition to myself have come to know that there is all the difference in the world between an experience of the Scriptures in which there is a word of God that seizes me and that experience in which I am simply seizing the words on the page—however interesting this latter may be in the work of scholarship. In the former case I find myself addressed, caught up in all of the individuality of my concrete existence by something beyond me. The action is from God to me in a distinctively personal manner. This is the common testimony across wide ranges of Christian fellowship and history and individual differences. I think it is this sense of being seized in the presence of the Scripture, in a manner common across the ages, that gives the Bible its power to assure us in the face of our fallibility.

Both in the experience of Scripture and of other things—circumstances, our own inner thoughts and impulses, the reading of history or biography—the word frequently comes in a way which approximates the experience of an *audible* voice. When examined closely, the data of Christian experience reveals that this is much more common than is generally thought. But the audibility of the voice is not anything essential to it, nor does it have any effect on the reliability of our experience of the voice. The essentials remain, once again, the distinctive quality, spirit, and content which we have learned through experience to associate with the personal presence of God.

Scholarship, both biblical and otherwise, certainly is important to the individual and to the Church as a whole. It is a part of our part in responsible living before God. But it can never stand in the place of experience of the living voice of God, and it also cannot remedy or remove our fallibility. In general, no person is dependent upon the expertise of biblical or other scholars for a saving and walking knowledge of God. Humble openness before the recorded Word of God is sufficient as the occasion of God's saving and guiding word to us. Those who know all *about* the Word of God may yet never have *heard* it, and those who have heard it and recognize it readily may have little to say about it. But we need many who both know it and know about it, that it might come to have freer course and more competent reception in the community of believers, and that God's guidance of His people might be more effective in realizing His purposes.

Practical Consequences

Knowing the voice of God, the *practical understanding* of that voice in our minds and hearts, is *not* a luxury to the people of God, not something to be allocated to those who like special spiritual high points. Let us consider four aspects of the importance of this understanding to life in God's Kingdom.

First of all, without this direct communication with Christ who is the Head of the Church, the rule of God will not be promoted through our lives as it should and could be. The understanding of the voice of God as here described gives *substance* to the relationship between Christ and His Church. *He talks to it,* and that is what it means for His word to live in the Church.

When we align ourselves with the Kingdom of Christ, when we come into the family of God, we are an outpost of that kingdom. If you wish, though these are crude metaphors, we have the telephone installed so that we can take the heavenly orders and participate in decisions as we do kingdom business. We have the computer terminal put in place, where we can communicate and act and interact with God in His work. It is important that we have God's instructions and directions for what we do. And it is not true that the Bible *alone,* or our subjective experiences *alone,* or the circumstances given to be interpreted, are going to give us the kind of guidance we need. It was never so intended. We must be spoken to by God, specifically and concretely guided in thought and action, to the extent and by the instrumentalities He chooses. We have in this book tried to make literal sense of what that might amount to.

But secondly, we as individuals must have the confidence and peace that comes from knowing that we are indeed in communication with God Himself.

Think of the benediction that contains the blessing of Moses (Num. 6:24-26): "The Lord bless thee, and keep thee." What does this mean? "The Lord make his face shine upon thee." What does that mean? Have you ever watched someone who loves another—as a little child, for example, loves its father—when the father's face was *not* lifted up on that child and shining upon it. Have you perhaps been in that place yourself? Do you remember what it was like to experience your father or mother turning away from you in anger and withdrawal, when their face did not shine, but scowled upon you or ignored you? Communication was cut off. You were agonized by it unless you learned to harden your heart against it. There is a communication and guidance that is absolutely necessary in order for us to have the kind of confidence and peace appropriate to a child of God.

A little child lost his mother to death. He could not be adequately consoled and continued to be troubled, especially at night. He would come into the room where the father was and ask to sleep with the father. This little child would never rest until he knew not only that he was with his father, but that the father's face turned toward him. He would ask in the dark, "Father, is your face turned toward me now?" And when at last assured of this, he was at peace and was able to go to sleep. How lonely life is! Oh, we can "get by" with a God who does not speak. Many apparently do. But it is not much of a life, and certainly not the life intended for us or the *abundant* life which Jesus Christ came to make available.

We love to sing the song, "This Is My Father's World." But in its words, for all their loveliness, there is no personal element. The song of the bird and the music of the spheres and the rustling of the grass to which it refers is an impersonal arrangement, though a glorious one. There is all the difference in the world between having a fine general view that this is our Father's world—or even that an "arrangement" has been made for our eternal redemption—and, by contrast, having experiential confidence that the Father's face, whether in the dark of the night or the brightness of the day, is turned to us, shining upon us, and that the Father is speaking to us individually.

Thirdly, it is important for us to know on a practiced, experiential basis how God speaks in order to *protect* ourselves and others within our concern. We all know, as previously discussed, what foolishness sometimes comes following the words, "God told me." Indeed, we all know not only what foolishness, but sometimes what horror, can come from those who say those words. We need to know what the voice of God is like, how it comes, and what kinds of things it might say in order to protect ourselves and those around us in the fellowship of the faithful from people who are being carried away with voices contrary to God, and which they themselves may not understand.

It is of vital importance that we be able to recognize when people in positions of power and authority do not, for all their authority, know what they are talking about, or are guided by evil. For our own protection we need to understand how God's voice works, as well as for the protection of those we love and the prosperity of the visible Church. Hence guidance has to be taken out of the realm of superstition and reduced to terms that everyone who wants to understand can understand.

Cult leaders can, without any exception, be clearly marked if what has been said above about the spirit and content of God's voice and God's leader is understood. The tragedy of Jim Jones and "Jonestown"—which we now know began long before Jonestown among the decent citizenry of the United States—could have been stopped dead in its tracks if but a few of the people he gathered around him had been in a position to see through his claims to speak for God. But they themselves had no competence in dealing with the voice of God as a practical, experiential matter, and through mystification of that voice and "spiritual" bullying were led to the slaughter. If those who pulled their "guidance" on others knew that they would have their guidance examined by compassionate but strong individuals who have understanding of such matters, things would go much better for our churches generally, and for the individuals in them.

But danger not only comes from the "wild side" of religion, it can also come from the respectable side. When, in the ninth chapter of John, Jesus healed a blind man on the Sabbath, the leaders of the people, proud of being Moses' disciples (v. 28), "knew" that Jesus could not possibly be of God because He did not observe their restrictions on working during the Sabbath (v. 16). They *knew* that this man was a sinner because they *knew* the Bible. And they *knew* that the Bible said that you were not supposed to do the kinds of things Jesus was doing on the Sabbath. Therefore, since this man Jesus did these kinds of things on the Sabbath, He was a sinner.

They had good, reliable general knowledge of how it was supposed to be. The man healed could only report: "Whether he be a sinner or no, I know not: one thing I know, that, whereas I was blind, now I see" (v. 25). But *that* was not "in the Bible," in the Law. They had *their* guidance and they thought that it was sufficient. But it was not sufficient, though very respectable, for it allowed them to condemn the power and works of love in Jesus Himself. Verse 29: "We know that God spoke to Moses; as for this fellow, we don't know where he is coming from."

"We don't know!" That is perhaps the most damning statement they could possibly have made about themselves. They looked at what Jesus did and said, "We don't know what this person is doing. We don't know where He is coming from. We don't know that He is of God." What they were really confessing was that they did not know who God is or what His works are. They in their own way shared Nicodemus's problem of not being able to see the Kingdom of God. And many stand in that same place today. They can look at the greatest works of love and, if those works do not conform to their legalistic ideas of, for example, what the Bible or the church teaches, or their ideas of what their subjective experiences teach, they can condemn them without a wink, "We *know* that this is wrong."

We really have no recourse, no place to stand in the face of the mad religionist on the one hand, or the blind legalist on the other, if we do not have firsthand knowledge of individualized guidance held safely within a community of brothers and sisters in Christ who also have such knowledge of God's personal dealings with the soul.[17]

Fourthly and finally, experience and understanding of God's voice to us can alone make the events of the Bible real to us and allow our faith in the truth of the Bible to rise beyond mere abstract conviction that it *must* be true. This is a theme which we have already touched upon a number of times. But it is so important that we must return to it once again.

Consider, for example, the events recorded in 1 Samuel 16:1-13. This is the story of the selection of David as king over Israel. As with so much of the Bible, the passage is filled with "the Lord said to . . . ," and in this case to Samuel. "The Lord said unto Samuel, How long wilt thou mourn for Saul, seeing I have rejected him from reigning over Israel? fill thine horn with oil, and go, I will send thee to Jesse the Bethlehemite: for I have provided me a king among his sons. And Samuel said, How can I go? if Saul hear it, he will kill me. And the Lord said, Take an heifer with thee, and say, I am come to sacrifice to the Lord. And call Jesse to the sacrifice, and I will shew thee what thou shalt do: and thou shalt anoint unto me him whom I name unto thee " (vv. 1-3).

When the sons of Jesse came before Samuel, the first was Eliab. And apparently Eliab was a fine looking person, for Samuel said, "Surely the Lord's anointed is before him." But the Lord said to Samuel, in words which should always remain before us, "Look not on his countenance, or on the height of his stature; because I have refused him: for the Lord seeth not as man seeth; for man looketh on the outward appearance, but the Lord looketh on the heart" (v. 7).

Abinadab, Shammah and all of Jesse's other sons besides David, who was not present, then passed before Samuel with the same result. Finally, David was called out of the fields where he was keeping the sheep. And when he came before Samuel, "The Lord said, Arise, anoint him: for this is he. Then Samuel took the horn of oil, and anointed him in the midst of his brethren: and the spirit of the Lord came upon David from that day forward" (vv. 12-13).

It is essential to the strength of our faith that we be in some measure capable of inwardly identifying with Samuel's experience as he conversed with the Lord in the midst of Jesse's family.

David's own conversational interactions with God are documented at many points in the Bible, but at none more graphically than in 1 Chronicles 14. After he had assumed the throne of Israel, the Philistines came to war against him. David then "inquired of God" (v. 10) what he should do. This was probably done by standing before the Ark of God, which had been used earlier in the history of Israel for such inquiry, and which had been recently relocated by David in an effort to place it in Jerusalem, which he had chosen as his capital city (see 1 Chron. 13). "And David inquired of God, saying, Shall I go up against the Philistines? and wilt thou deliver them into mine hand? And the Lord said unto him, Go up; for I will deliver them into thine hand" (v. 10).

And so it came to pass. The Philistines then regrouped and later set themselves in array in the same valley. "Therefore David inquired again of God; and God said unto him, Go not up after them; turn away from them, and come upon them over against the mulberry trees. And it shall be, when thou shalt hear a sound of going in the tops of the mulberry trees, that then thou shalt go out to battle; for God is gone forth before thee to smite the host of the Philistines" (vv. 14-15). And it occurred just as God said.

Now one of the most interesting things about these cases, and the many similar passages which the Bible contains, is the specific information, the clear and detailed *cognitive content* given in the movement of God upon the minds of Samuel and David. What we have here are not mere "impressions," "impulsions," or "feelings" which are so commonly thought to be what God gives in guiding man. Rather, we have a specific and full cognitive or "propositional" content concerning what is the case, what is to be done, and what will happen. David and Samuel are not left to wonder what their "impulses" to do this or that or their "feelings" about this or that mean; nor do they have to test them against the Scripture or circumstances. They are *told.* David does not have to speculate about the meaning of "the sound of going in the tops of the mulberry trees." He is *told.*

It is possible to talk about conscious guidance in terms of mysterious feelings, curious circumstances, and special scriptural nuances of meaning to the point where God's very character is called into question. He is not a mumbling trickster. By contrast, it is to be expected, given the revelation of God in Christ, that *if* there is something He would have us know, He will be both able and willing and will in fact plainly communicate it to us, if we are but open and prepared by our experience to hear and obey. This is *exactly* what takes place in the lives of such biblical characters as we have just seen.

The very "mechanism" of inspiration—through which

"the prophecy came not in old time by the will of man: but holy men of God spake as they were moved by the Holy Ghost" (2 Pet. 1:21), and through which "all scripture is given by inspiration [or breathing] of God" (2 Tim. 3:16)—is, on its human side, nothing but thought and perception of that distinctive character which its subjects had come, through experience, to recognize as the voice of God in their own souls. The thoughts and perceptions were indeed *their* thoughts and perceptions—it could not be otherwise—but bore within themselves the unmistakable stamp of divine quality, intent, and origination.

Thus we find Paul very nicely distinguishing between what the Lord said in him and what he was saying on his own (1 Cor. 7:12). Yet when he composed his letters under divine inspiration *he* did not stop thinking or set aside his perceptions and feelings, becoming an unconscious writer or mindless voice box. His thoughts and perceptions were his, but God's also, and recognized to be such by Paul in virtue of the distinctive character which he knew so well and worked with in utter confidence.

And when we by our experiences and deliberations have learned to recognize the voice of God as it enters into the texture of *our* souls, the lives of biblical personalities become real to us, the life of God in them becomes something we can identify with, and our faith rises to claim our portion in the unified reign of God in His people throughout history and in heaven and on earth.

Questions

1. What are the "three lights" referred to in this chapter and what problems arise because of their interdependence?

2. What are the "three factors of voice" treated in this chapter? Which is the most reliable? Why?

3. Does the lack of an "audible" quality diminish the reliability of that experience of voice? Why?

4. "Any voice which promises total exemption from suffering and failure is most certainly *not* God's word." True or false? Discuss the "spiritual panacea" problem.

5. How can you recognize the voice of Satan?

6. Do you agree with the author's view of "infallibility"? Why? What are the practical implications of *your* view?

7. What are the four practical consequences of knowing God's voice which are treated in this chapter?

8. There is a distinction between approaching the Bible as an object of "scholarship" and as a place to experience the living voice of God. Is that distinction (a) clear? (b) useful? (c) problematical?

9. Ability at recognizing the "voice of God" serves as protection against cultic leaders on both the "wild side" and "respectable side" of religion. Illustrate and discuss.

Notes

1. G. Campbell Morgan, *God's Perfect Will* (Grand Rapids: Baker Book House, 1978), p. 157.

2. It is possible to understand the teaching of the sufficiency of the anointing in various ways, but no biblical Christian can *deny* it. Since the flood-tide of European mysticism in the thirteenth and fourteenth centuries (see *Master Eckhart and the Rhineland Mystics,* by Jeanne Ancelet-Hustache [Harper Torchbooks, no date] for a good introduction) this teaching has been nowhere more strongly defended than by the Quakers or Friends; and their best presentation is in Propositions I, II and III of *An Apology for the True Christian Divinity,* written by Robert Barclay (many editions). I believe that, on the whole, a more correct view of the relationship between the Bible and the anointing is given in William Law, John Wesley, and Andrew Murray. For Murray see especially *The*

Spirit of Christ (London, James Nisbet, 1899, and other editions). For Wesley, see the various discourses on the Spirit and especially on the witness of the Spirit, in the standard edition of his sermons. For Law, see *The Power of the Spirit,* already referred to, as well as his *Serious Call to a Devout and Holy Life* (many editions).

3. F.B. Meyer, *The Secret of Guidance* (Chicago: Moody Press, n.d.).

4. Ibid., p. 18.

5. See also Bob Mumford, *Take Another Look at Guidance: Discerning the Will of God* (Plainfield, NJ: Logos International, 1971), ch. 7; and G. Campbell Morgan, *God's Perfect Will* (Grand Rapids: Baker Books, 1980), pp. 155f.

6. Beth Spring, "What the Bible Means," *Christianity Today,* December 17, 1982, pp. 45-48.

7. William Law, *The Power of the Spirit* (Fort Washington, PA: Christian Literature Crusade, 1971), p. 61.

8. Don Ihde, *Listening and Voice* (Athens, OH: Ohio University Press, 1976).

9. E. Stanley Jones, *A Song of Ascents* (Nashville: Abingdon Press, 1979), p. 190.

10. John Wesley, *Sermons on Several Occasions* (New York: B. Waugh and T. Mason, 1836), vol. 1, pp. 91-92.

11. Adela Rogers St. John, *Guideposts,* December, 1968, p. 8.

12. Mumford, *Take Another Look at Guidance,* pp. 85-86.

13. J. Edwin Orr, "What Made the Welsh Revival 'Extraordinary,' " *The Forerunner,* vol. 2, no. 8, p. 11.

14. Isaac Watts, "Am I a Soldier of the Cross?"

15. Meyer, *Secret of Guidance,* p. 31.

16. John Bunyan, *Grace Abounding to the Chief of Sinners* (Grand Rapids: Baker Books, 1981), pp. 46-47.

17. The communal side of guidance is not studied in this book, but we refer the reader to chapter 12 of Richard Foster's *Celebration of Discipline* (New York: Harper and Row, 1978), pp. 150-162.

CHAPTER 9

GUIDANCE AND BEYOND: A LIFE MORE THAN GUIDANCE

> *To deliver the soul from the sin which is its ruin and bestow on it the holiness which is its health and peace, is the end of all God's dealings with His children; and precisely because He cannot merely give, but must enable us to attain it ourselves, if we are really to have the liberty of His children, the way He must take is long and arduous" (John Wood Oman).*[1]

> *So likewise ye, when ye shall have done all those things which are commanded you, say, We are unprofitable servants: we have done that which was our duty to do (Luke 17:10).*

In the foregoing chapters we have dealt with many aspects of divine guidance which might seem remote, scholarly, or merely philosophical. It is an unavoidable fact, however, that what we understand or do not understand, believe and do not believe in any area of our lives, governs our practice or action with an iron hand. Contrary to what many may believe, this does not cease to be true when we enter the realm of the religious life. Misunderstandings and mistaken beliefs about guidance, or more generally about God and communications between Him and His creatures, make impossible a right walk with Him. This is no less true if we "don't want to think about it." I have seen repeatedly confirmed, in often tragic cases, the dire consequences of refusing to give deep, thoughtful consideration to the ways in which God chooses to deal with us.

Indeed, refusal to make the effort to understand God's dealings with mankind, to study the Bible and whatever else may help us to understand it, is rebellion against the express will of God who commands us to love Him with *all our mind,* as well as with all our heart, soul, and strength (Mark 12:30). We can therefore say on scriptural grounds that it is the direct and general will of God that we *study* His ways of guiding and communicating with us. The willful rejection of thoughtful and careful study is not faith, and it does not spring from faith. It is the rejection of the God-appointed means to God-appointed ends.

But now that we have made the study, endured the hardship of thinking carefully and in depth about divine guidance in our world, and about the presentation of it given within the Scriptures, we must bring our results to bear upon the life which any serious disciple of Christ consciously undertakes to lead from day to day. If the foregoing chapters have been successful, we are now in a position to bring those who are concerned to know God's will *for them* into a place of rest and assurance where they can be confident that the Lord's face does indeed shine upon them.

The question which we will deal with in this final chapter is, then, essentially a how-to question: How may we come to live confidently and in a sensible fashion with God as a conversational presence in our lives? This leads on to subordinate questions such as: How far can we *count on* guidance being given? What does it mean when it is not given, and what then are we to do?

In Summary

In answering these questions, we start out from a brief *summary of fundamental points* elaborated in the course of this book.

While God's communications, including those intended to guide our specific choices, come through experiences of many kinds, the *content* or *meaning* of His specific and individualized communications to us always finally takes the form of the "inner voice," without which the accompanying events, appearances, or biblical passages remain objects of puzzlement, mystification, and conjecture.

God may of course guide us "mechanically" without *addressing* us and guiding us through our own understandings and choices, as we guide our automobile without speaking to it. But whenever He guides us in conscious cooperation with Him as our friend and co-worker, He does so by speaking to us: by giving to us thoughts and perceptions which bear within themselves the marks of their divine origination. This "speaking" most commonly occurs in conjunction with study of and reflection upon the Bible, the written Word of God, wherever the Bible is effectively available.

Our ability to recognize the voice of God, and to distinguish it with practical certainty from all else that shows up there, is acquired by effort and experimentation, both on God's part and ours. It does not come "automatically" by divine imposition and fiat. Those who *really* want to live under God's guidance—and who by proper teaching or other special provision made by God become convinced that He will, and perhaps *is,* speaking to *them*—can proceed to learn through a course of experience what is the quality, the spirit, and the content of God's voice. They will then distinguish and understand the voice of God, not infallibly, but *at least* as clearly and with as much accuracy as they do the voice of any other person with whom they are on intimate terms.

We emphasize once again that this does *not* mean that they will always correctly understand what God says to them, or even that it will be *easy* for them to get the message straight. One great cause of confusion about divine guidance is that people make infallibility a condition of guidance. It helps, I believe and hope, to understand that guidance is communication, and communication occurs constantly where infallibility is completely out of the question. Even infallibility of the speaker—as in the case where it is God who is speaking—does not and need not guarantee infallibility of the hearer. But communication also reliably occurs where the speakers are not perfect. I well know my children's voices and would recognize them under a very wide range of circumstances. Generally I understand what they say. But I would know it was they who were speaking even if I could not understand what they said.

Indeed, careful study of personal relationships shows that recognition of a certain voice is often the cue for one to *stop* listening, or even for one to distort the message in specific ways that are tied in to the nature of the relationship between the people involved. I am convinced that this often happens in the divine/human conversation, and it almost always happens when God speaks to those who are in out-and-out rebellion against Him. One of the deepest teachings of Jesus concerned the manner in which we hear, and the fact that some people do not have ears simply to hear, except for certain other purposes—such as to filter and manage the message the better to fit their own lives and purposes:

"If any man have ears to hear, let him hear. And he said unto them, Take heed what ye hear: with what measure ye mete, it shall be measured to you; and unto you that hear shall more be given . . . . And with many such parables spake he the word unto them, as they were able to hear it" (Mark 4:23-24,33).

Listening is an *active* process which may select or omit from, as well as reshape, the message intended by the one speaking. It and all our ways of perceiving turn out to be fundamental displays of our character, of our freedom and our bondages. If we really do *not want* God's guidance over our lives, then—no matter what we may *say*—that fact will position us before God in such a manner "that seeing they may see, and not perceive; and hearing they may hear, and not understand; lest at any time they should be converted, and their sins should be forgiven them" (Mark 4:12). If we do *not want* to be converted from our chosen and habitual ways, our very perceptual mechanisms will filter out the voice of God or twist it to our purposes.

The doleful fact is that very few human beings really do want God's guidance in their lives. This is shown by how rarely we look for it when we are not in trouble or faced with a decision which we do not know how to handle. Persons who understand and warmly desire God's guidance will, by contrast, be as concerned to have it when they are not facing trouble or big decisions as when they are. This is a test which we should all apply to ourselves as we go in search of guidance. It may reveal that our failure to get guidance when we want it is due to the fact that we do not in general want God to guide us except when "we need it." Experience shows that many who want God's guidance when in trouble cannot find it, or at least have no assurance that they have found it. This is because they do not first and foremost simply want God's guidance. They at heart only want to get out of trouble or make the decisions which will be best for them. Indeed, I have spoken with many who think of divine guidance *only* as something to get and keep them out of trouble.

Our lack of desire for God's guidance merely for itself is also shown by a disregard of the *plain* directives in the Scriptures. Sanctification from sexual uncleanness (1

Thess. 4:3) and a continuously thankful heart (1 Thess. 5:18) are among the many things set forth as guidance to *all* persons. It is utter foolishness to disregard these plain directives and then expect to be given *special* guidance.

We do not mean to say that God absolutely will not, in His mercy, guide and communicate with those who have departed from the general guidance He has given. Contrary to the well-meaning words of the blind man whom Jesus healed (John 9:31), God does, upon occasion, "hear sinners." But this cannot be *counted on* or be part of a regular and intelligible *plan* for living in a conversational relationship with God. Anyone who rejects the general counsels of Scripture is in fact planning *not* to be guided by God, and cannot then count on being able to *use* God's guidance on particular occasions to deliver them from their perplexities.

However, the person who honestly desires God's guidance for its own sake and the glory of God, and who, as a part of his total plan for living in harmony with God, adopts the general counsels of Scripture as the framework within which he is to know His daily graces—*that* person will most assuredly receive God's specific conscious guidance to him through the inner voice to the extent that such guidance is appropriate in developing his conformation to Jesus Christ. There *is* a limit to which such guidance is appropriate, and we will return to this point in what follows. But it is in general true, as G. Campbell Morgan has written, that "Wherever there are hearts waiting for the Voice of God, that Voice is to be heard."[2]

With this summation of what we have learned from our studies before us, we turn now to deal with our concluding practical questions.

Listening for God

Dr. James Dobson has given some of the best practical advice I have ever heard on how the person who really wants the will of God and has a basically correct understanding should proceed. Describing how he himself does it, he says: "I get down on my knees and say, 'Lord I need to know what you want me to do, and I am listening. Please speak to me through my friends, books, and magazines I pick up and read, and through circumstances.' "[3] The simplicity of this should not mislead us. When we are in a proper functioning relationship with our Lord it is exactly what we are to do. And then we are, as Dr. Dobson says, to *listen.* This means that we pay a special kind of attention both to what is going on within us and to our surrounding circumstances. It is good to keep this simple prayer for guidance before us and to observe regular times for listening. Again we call on F.B. Meyer:

> Be still each day for a short time, sitting before God in meditation, and ask the Holy Spirit to reveal to you the truth of Christ's indwelling. Ask God to be pleased to make known to *you* what is the riches of the glory of this mystery (Col. 1:27).[4]

If we have this general habit then, when alerted to the need for particular guidance, we will be enabled to listen for *it* with greater patience, confidence, and acuity.

What I find personally to work best is, after asking for guidance in the manner indicated, to devote the next hour or so to some kind of activity which neither obsesses my attention with other things nor allows me to be intensely focused upon the matter in question. Housework or gardening, driving about on errands or paying bills will do. I have learned not to worry about whether or not this is "going to work." I know that it does not *have to* work, but I am sure that it *will* work if God has something He really wants me to know or do. This is because I know how great and good He is. Usually by the end of an hour or so there has stood forth within my consciousness an idea or thought with that peculiar character of quality and spirit and content that I have come to associate with God's voice. If so, I may then decide to discuss the matter with others, usually without informing them that "God has told me," or I may decide to reconsider the matter in the same way after some period of time. But if nothing emerges by the end of the hour, I am not alarmed. I set myself to hold the matter before the Lord as I go about my business, and confidently get on with my life. Very often within a day something happens through which God's voice is heard. If it does not, I generally cease specifically to seek guidance on the matter in question. But I am neither disappointed nor alarmed nor even concerned, as a rule, and I shall explain why as we proceed further. (Let us be clear that we are not speaking here of prayer generally, where a different approach of greater persistence and tenacity is often called for.)

My own experience, and what I have learned from others who clearly have signed their lives over to God and learned to work with His voice, leads me to believe that direction will always be made available to the mature disciple if without it serious harm may befall persons concerned or the cause of Christ. The obedient, listening heart, mature in the things of God, will in such a case find the voice plain and the message clear after the fashion of those experiences of the friends of God recorded in the Bible. This is a claim which any person can test by experience if he is willing to meet the conditions.

Guidance Is Not a Gimmick

Of course, God often speaks without any such procedure of seeking His individualized word as just described. And we must not be misled by anyone into thinking that there is a some sure-fire *method* for squeezing what we want to know out of God. A life surrendered to God, a humble openness to His direction even when it is contrary to our wants and assumptions, experience with the way His word comes to us, and fervent but patient requests for guidance do not constitute a method for getting an answer from Him. Once again we must say, guidance is not a gimmick. Talk of "method" is, strictly speaking, out of place here, although we may lay down general practical guidelines. After all, God is not something we work up for a result, even though certain ways of behaving in relation to Him are more or less appropriate.

We must, above all, beware of trying to *force* guidance from God. This is especially true right when it is most likely to be attempted. That is, when we are not in peaceful union with Him. Saul, first king of Israel, poignantly illustrates the folly of such attempts. He certainly did not above all want to wait upon God and see His will done. To keep control over his armies in the face of the Philistines he did not wait as he ought to have for Samuel the priest to arrive, but he went ahead himself, even though it was not his office, and made peace offerings and burnt offerings (1 Sam. 13:5-10).

When Samuel at last arrived, he asked Saul why he had done this. The reply goes to the very heart of Saul's character: "Because I saw that the people were scattered from me, and that thou camest not within the days appointed, and that the Philistines gathered themselves together at Michmash; therefore said I, The Philistines will come down now upon me to Gilgal, and I have not made supplication unto the Lord; I forced myself therefore, and offered a burnt offering" (vv. 11-12). Samuel immediately announced that Saul would lose his kingdom (vv. 13-14), for he clearly saw that Saul was a man who would take things into his hands to get his own way and that he also would find a "good reason" for doing so.

A little later Saul disobeyed again and found a "good reason" when he did not utterly destroy Amalek (1 Sam. 15). He even pretended to Samuel to have obeyed (v. 13), and when his deceit was uncovered he blamed his disobedience upon "the people" (v. 24). Again Samuel announced that the kingdom would be taken from Saul (v. 26).

Finally, Saul comes to his extremity, facing death. Samuel himself was dead by that time, and "when Saul inquired of the Lord, the Lord answered him not, neither by dreams: nor by Urim, nor by prophets" (1 Sam. 28:6). Now, as was his way, Saul would *force* God to speak to him. Even though he himself had banned witches from Israel, he sought out a witch and compelled her to call up the spirit of Samuel (vv. 7-11) to tell him what to do. Samuel arose "out of the earth" (v. 13) and said to Saul, "Why has thou disquieted me, to bring me up?" (v. 15). Then Saul poured out his tale of woe: "The Philistines make war against me, and God is departed from me, and answereth me no more, neither by prophets, nor by dreams: therefore I have called thee, that thou mayest *make known unto me what I shall do*" (v. 15, italics added).

How pitifully typical this is of the human view of God and His guidance! He is treated as a celestial aspirin to cure the headaches brought on by the steady, willful tendency of our lives away from and even against Him, a cosmic butler to clean up our messes. Gimmicks and tricks suited only to idols are sought to compel *Him* to serve *us*!

Samuel then read Saul's sentence to him: "Wherefore, then, dost thou ask of me, seeing the Lord is departed from thee, and is become thine enemy? . . . Tomorrow shalt thou and thy sons be with me: the Lord also shall deliver the host of Israel into the hands of the Philistines" (vv. 16,19). At these words Saul fell flat upon the earth, weakened by hunger and terror. God would no longer be used by him.

Deciding "On Your Own"

And with this we come to what is perhaps one of the greatest problems for the devout person's attempts to understand guidance. Even if we are not in disobedience to God, even if our hearts are perfectly attuned to His will, there will be many times in which no particularized guidance will come from God concerning what we are to do.

We must not then automatically assume that if God does not guide us in a particular matter we are displeasing to Him. *If* that is the cause—which of course is possible—there will be ways of finding this out other than raising a particular matter to see whether or not He will guide us. It will be something that can be discovered and clearly known if we but seek it out. Remember, God will not play little games of hide-and-seek with us. Here, as earlier stressed, it is all important to believe that He is the kind of person revealed by Jesus. Such a person will show us what the problem is, if there is a problem, provided we sincerely and with an open mind pray to be shown. He is not frivolous, is not coy, will not torture us. In our relationship with Him there is no mysterious "catch" to guidance, no riddle to solve, no incantation to get just right. Not with the God and Father of our Lord Jesus Christ!

But there are other reasons than His displeasure why a specific word may not be forthcoming to guide us in particular circumstances. In general, it is the will of God that we ourselves should have a great part in determining our path through life. This does not mean that He is not with us. God both develops and tests our character by leaving us to decide. He calls us to responsible citizenship in His kingdom by—in effect or reality—saying, as often as possible: MY WILL FOR YOU IS FOR YOU TO DECIDE ON YOUR OWN.

In his profound chapter on "The Will of God," John Wood Oman gives us this excellent statement of the point:

> The practical effect of reconciliation to God is thus to find ourselves in an order of life which is our succor, so far beyond our own contriving and for ends so far above our own conceiving, that we have no concern except to serve in it. Practically, as well as theoretically, we, thereby, attain such a perfect unity of morality and religion that we can only be absolutely dependent

> upon God as we are absolutely independent in our own souls, and only absolutely independent in our own souls as we are absolutely dependent on God. A saved soul, in other words, is a soul true to itself because, with its mind on God's will of love and not on itself, it stands in God's world unbribable and undismayed, having freedom as it has piety and piety as it is free.[5]

It is thus that there rings out from the Apostle Paul and the saints through the ages that robust and powerful: "I live; yet not I, but Christ liveth in me" (Gal. 2:19).

A child *cannot* develop into a responsible, competent human being if it is always told what to do. Personality and character is in its very essence inner directedness. This inner directedness is perfected in redemption. That is Oman's point. Moreover, a child's character cannot be known—even to itself—until it is turned loose to do *what it wants.* It is precisely what it wants that manifests the person it is.

What we want, what we think, what we decide to do when the voice of God does not come—or, also, when we have so immersed ourselves in Him that His voice within us is not held in distinction from our own thoughts and perceptions—shows *who we are,* either God's mature children, friends, and co-workers, or something less.

There is, after all, a *neurotic, faithless,* and *irresponsible* seeking of God's will: a kind of spiritual hypochondria, always taking its own spiritual temperature, far more concerned with being righteous than with loving God and others and doing and enjoying what is good. There *is* such a thing as being righteous overmuch (Eccl. 7:16). We may insist upon God telling us what to do because we are obsessed with *being right.* But we may also do it because we do not really have a hearty faith in His gracious goodwill toward us. If so, we need to grow up.

We may in our heart of hearts suspect that God is

mean and tyrannical and therefore be afraid to make a move without dictation from Him. So far from honoring God, such an attitude is blasphemous, idolatrous, and certain to prevent us from ever entering into that conversational relationship with God wherein sensible guidance is given as is appropriate and is clearly revealed and reliably understood. How much would you have to do with a person who harbored such opinions about you?

The "Perfect" Will of God

The children of God cannot be groveling robots or obsequious and cringing sycophants and also be *the children of God!* For such creatures could never bear the family resemblance. A son or daughter is not the father's toady, and toadying is no part of either humility or worship before the God and Father of Jesus Christ. "The humility that cringes in order that reproof may be escaped or favor obtained is as unchristian as it is profoundly immoral."[6]

In this context we need to say something about being in the *perfect* will of God. If our lives conform to the general counsels of God for His people, as given to us in the written Word as a whole, then we are perfectly in God's general or moral will. If, in addition, we have received and obeyed specific guidance by a specific word of God to us concerning a particular matter, then we are perfectly in God's specific will for us relevant to that matter.

But suppose no such specific word has come to us concerning some matter of great importance in our lives. (Should we enter this school or that? Live here or there? etc.) Does this mean that in the matter at hand we *cannot* be in God's perfect will, or that we can be so only by chance, following some anxiety-ridden guessing game about "what God wants me to do"?

Most assuredly it does not. We must resolutely resist the tendency *automatically* to blame the absence of guidance upon our own wrongness, and we must equally deny that the absence of guidance necessarily means that we are not quite right in something less than God's *perfect* will. If we are living in sincere devotion to the fulfillment of God's purposes in us, we can be sure that the God who stood forth in Jesus Christ will not mumble and tease and trick us regarding any specific matter He wants done. We cannot too often reemphasize this point, since the tendency otherwise is so strong and ever present. Think of it this way: No decent parent would obfuscate his or her intent for their children. A general principle for interpreting the behavior of God toward us is provided in Jesus' words, "If ye then, being evil, know how to give good gifts unto your children: how much more shall your heavenly Father give the Holy Spirit to them that ask him?" (Luke 11:13). How much more shall your heavenly Father give clear instructions to them that ask Him in those cases where He has any to give? And where He has none to give, then whatever lies within His moral will and is undertaken in faith *is His perfect will.* It is no less perfect merely because it was not precisely dictated by Him. Indeed, it is perhaps more perfect just because there was no need of His dictation. He expects and trusts us to choose, and goes with us in our choice.

Many different things, then, may *each* be His perfect will in a given circumstance. We should assume that this is so in all cases where we are walking in His general will, are experienced in hearing His voice, and find no specific direction given. In these cases there are various things which would equally please God though He directs none of them in particular to be done. All are "perfect" in His will because there is none better than the others and all are good.

In his book earlier referred to, *Decision Making and the Will of God,* Garry Friesen has done a masterful job of critiquing the view that God always has *one* particular thing for you to do in a given case, and that correct decision making depends upon your "finding out" what *that* thing is. If you miss it you will only be in God's "permissive" will at best, and a second-class citizen in the Kingdom of God. Against this extremely harmful view he remarks:

> The *major point* is this: God does not have an ideal, detailed life-plan uniquely designed for each believer that must be discovered in order to make correct decisions. The concept of an "individual will of God" cannot be established by reason, experience, biblical example or biblical teaching.[7]

So the *perfect* will of God may allow, for a particular person, a number of different alternatives. For most people, for example, a number of different mates (or none at all), various vocations, educational institutions, or places of residence *may all* equally be God's perfect will, none being in themselves "better" or preferred by God in relation to the ultimate outcome desired by Him. And the sincere seeker should assume that this is so, and move forward with faith in God if no specific guidance comes on the matter concerned after a reasonable period of time. All of this is consistent with there *sometimes* being only one choice which would perfectly fulfill God's will for us. Our choices must be approached on a case-by-case basis just as life is lived one day at a time, trusting God.

Now just as character is revealed only when we are permitted or required to do as we want, so the degree and maturity of our faith are manifested only where no specific command is given. It is not the great and mature faith which merely does what it is told; rather such a faith, as William Carey said in going out as a pioneer missionary to India, "attempts great things for God, and expects great things from God." It moves to the work to be done, to the life to be lived, confident in the good-hearted companionship of the Father, Son, and Holy Spirit. Its vision of God and experience in His ways excludes obsessive anxiety about doing the right thing. Its confidence is not in guidance but in the Lord who is with us.

Caught in a Cosmic Conflict

But there is not only the case where we merely do not have guidance because our Father wishes us to decide. There is also the case when we are face-to-face with the powers of darkness that inhabit our universe along with us. How many people have fallen under some affliction and have cast about desperately to find out what they did wrong. Often it was nothing. Or whatever wrong they may have done was not responsible for their problem. We live in a universe in which there is a battle going on. As we live in that universe and share in God's creativity, both of creation and redemption, there are moments when we *stand alone.* Christ knew what that was. You will remember how He speaks in Luke 22:53 of the time when *His* hour would come—the hour of darkness, the hour of the powers of evil. In that hour He cried out, "My God, my God, why hast thou forsaken me?" (Matt. 27:46). You are going to face these hours and I am going to face them as well—even though in some sense, I believe, we will never be *utterly* forsaken and alone. Divine guidance, no matter how well we know it, will not spare us these times as it did not spare Him. Our faith is that they too "work together for good" for those who love God and are called according to His purposes (Rom. 8:28). In that we rest.

Greater Than Guidance

There is *something even greater* than always knowing what is the right thing to do and always being guided by the present hand of God. Paul brought this out very clearly in 1 Corinthians 13. He there spoke of knowledge, of prophecy, and of many other great things which we might find desirable. But he said that all of *these* are only partial and incomplete goods. The three greatest things—truly inseparable from each other when properly understood—

are faith, hope, and love. In the hour of darkness, even these three remained with Christ. *Faith, hope, and love.* The great height of our development as the disciples of Christ is not that we should always be having guidance, but that we should have been trained under the hand of God in such a way that we are able *to stand even without guidance* at our appointed time and place in faith, hope, and love. "And having done all, to stand" (Eph. 6:13)!

I can be assured, at a certain point in my progression toward spiritual maturity, simply that "he that sent me is with me: the Father hath not left me alone; for I do always those things that please him" (John 8:29). It should be the hope and *plan* of every disciple of Christ to come by gracious assistance to this *place of rest* in God's companionship and service. We will then, as Brother Lawrence advises, "not always scrupulously confine ourselves to certain rules, or particular forms of devotion, but act with a general confidence in God, with love and humility."[8] We will simply "stand fast in the liberty wherewith Christ hath made us free" (Gal. 5:1), not using the liberty as an opportunity for the flesh, but as the arena within which we "by love serve one another" (Gal. 5:13) just *because* "he that sent me is with me." The branch then abides in the vine, and the branch and the vine share a common life and together bear abundant fruit (John 15:1-8).

Never Beyond Risk

Now it is absolutely essential to the nature of personal maturation that we venture and be placed at risk. This truth is not withdrawn when we come to our walk with God. It will be clear, therefore, that we must disagree with very wise people who say that God's guidance *precludes* risk:

> One great law for all would be truly led by God's pillar of cloud and fire, is to take no step at the bidding of self-will or without the clear moving

> of the heavenly guide. Though the direction be new and the way seem beset with difficulty, there is never any risk provided we are only led of God. Each new advance needs separate and special authority from Him, and yesterday's guidance is not sufficient for today.[9]

Although much that is true and good is said here, it will be clear that we must disagree with it as a completely general plan for living with God's guidance in our lives. Much of the deplorable immaturity in the lives of Christians is due to adopting the general attitude expressed in this statement as the *whole* truth about divine guidance.

Beyond Guidance . . . Life and Rest!

Here we return once again to the themes which emerged in earlier parts of this book and have been touched on again and again. Divine guidance will never make sense except when set within a larger life of a certain kind. To try to locate divine guidance within human existence in its alienation from God is to return to idolatry where God is *for our use.* We must stand *beyond* the question of guidance in a life greater than our own, that of the kingdom of God. Our concern for guidance must be overwhelmed and lost in our worship and adoration of God and in our delight with His creation and His redemptive provision. Our aim in such a life is to identify all that we are and do with God's purpose in creating us and our world. Thus, we learn how to do all things to the glory of God (1 Cor. 10:31). That is, we come in all things to think and act so that His goodness and greatness and beauty will be as obvious as possible.

Once this point is secured, guidance can and will come in the extent and manner God deems suitable. And it will come without threat to the full participation of the redeemed self as a unique individual in the work of God. For those who come to this point, their life will be *theirs*—

irreducibly, preciously so—and yet God's; and through them will flow God's life, which is yet theirs. *This* is the life beyond and yet inclusive of guidance. It is the life which has its rise in the "additional" birth and culminates in the everlasting glorious society of heaven.

With this life in view John Wesley answered an intelligent and serious man who asked him: "I hear that you preach to a great number of people every night and morning. Pray what would you do with them? Whither would you lead them? What religion do you preach? What is it good for?" Honest and searching questions, which no minister should allow out of his mind. Wesley replied:

> I do preach to as many as desire to hear, every night and morning. You ask, what I would do with them: I would make them virtuous and happy, easy in themselves and useful to others. Whither would I lead them? To heaven; to God the Judge, the lover of all, and to Jesus the mediator of the New Covenant. What religion do I preach? The religion of love; the law of kindness brought to light by the gospel. What is this good for? To make all who receive it enjoy God and themselves: to make them all like God; lovers of all; contented in their lives; and crying out at their death, in calm assurance, "O grave, where is thy victory! Thanks be unto God, who giveth me the victory, through my Lord Jesus Christ."[10]

Within *such* a life, then, divine guidance is to be reliably and safely sought and found, free of mystification, gimmickry, hysteria, self-righteousness, self-exaltation, self-obsession, and dogmatism. On the presupposition of such a life, we can lay down a formula for living with guidance. It is *not* a formula for getting guidance out of God on all matters which may concern us. Any such a formula is ruled out by the very nature of God and of our relationship to Him, as explained above. It is, to repeat, a formula for *living with* guidance in a life surrendered and quickened to maturity by God.

The first two steps in the formula may be described as "foundational," since they only provide the basis for individualized guidance, but do not concern it only or specifically.

Foundational Steps

1. We have entered into the "additional" life by the additional birth, and so far as lies in our understanding and conscious will, we plan and make provision to *do* what we know to be morally right and what we know to be explicitly commanded by God. This commitment includes the intention *to find out* what may be morally right or commanded by God, and hence to grow in our knowledge.

2. We seek the *fullness* of the new life in Christ at the impulse of the Spirit of God in service to the good wherever it may appear, venturing beyond our powers in reliance upon God's upholding. Thus we move from faith to more faith as we find Him faithful. Above all we venture in the proclamation of the gospel of Jesus Christ and His Kingdom.

Guidance-Specific Steps

3. We meditate constantly upon God's principles for life as set forth in the Scriptures, always striving to penetrate more deeply into their meaning and into their applicability for our lives.

"This book of the law shall not depart out of thy mouth; but thou shalt meditate therein day and night, that thou mayest observe to do according to all that is written therein: for, then thou shalt make thy way prosperous, and then thou shalt have good success" (Josh. 1:8; see Ps. 1:1-3).

4. We are alert and attentive to what is happening in

our life and mind. It is there that God will address us, whatever the external occasion may be. Of the prodigal son it was said that he came *to himself* (Luke 15:17), and then he found the truth which was saving. When God came to Adam after he sinned He did not ask, "Adam, where is God?" but "Adam, where art *thou*?" (Gen. 3:9). We must purposefully, humbly, and intelligently cultivate the ability to listen and see what is happening in our own souls, and to recognize therein the movements of God.

5. We pray, speak to God constantly and specifically, about the matters which concern us. It is essential to our part of the conversation with God. You would not continue to speak to someone who did not talk with you, and you could not carry on a coherent conversation with someone who spoke to you rarely and on odd occasions only. The same is true of God. Nothing is too insignificant or hopeless to communicate with God about. Share all things with God by lifting them to Him in prayer, and ask for God's guidance, even—or perhaps especially—in those things which you think you already understand.

8. Listen on some such regular plan as described above. When God does speak to you, pay attention and receive it with *thanks*. It is a good habit to write such things down until you become so adept at the conversational relationship that you no longer need to. If it is an insight into truth that is given, dwell upon it, meditate upon it until you have thoroughly assimilated it. If it concerns action, carry it out in a suitable manner. God does not speak to us to amuse or entertain us, but to make some difference.

7. When God does *not* speak to you on the matter concerned:

   a. *Seek guidance about guidance.* Ask God to inform you if there is some hindrance *in you.* Be quiet and listen in the "inner forum" of your mind for any indication that you are blocking guidance. But do not endlessly pursue this. In prayer, set a specific length for this inquiry about guidance itself: normally no more than three days. Believe that if there is a problem, God will make it clear to you. Share the robust confidence of Abraham Lincoln, who said: "I am satisfied that, when the Almighty wants me to do, or not to do, a particular thing, He finds a way of letting me know it."

b. Counsel with at least two people whose relationship with God you respect, some of whom are *not* your "spiritual buddies." This may be done in a group setting if it does not concern an inherently private matter.

c. Act on *what seems best to you* after itemized consideration of the details of the alternatives. If alternatives seem equally desirable, then select one arbitrarily. This will rarely be necessary, but your confidence, remember, is in the Lord who goes with you, who is with His trusting children even when they blunder and flounder. You will here not know God in His guidance but in His faithfulness. "His compassions fail not. They are new every morning: great is thy faithfulness" (Lam. 3:22-23). These words were written by the prophet Jeremiah in a time of utter failure when the guiding hand of God was totally hidden from Israel and His punishing hand raised against them.

If we proceed in this way in quest of guidance, we will know God's guidance as a familiar personal fact which we can both comfortably live with and effectively introduce others into. We will know when God speaks and when He does not. We will know what to do when God speaks; and when He does not speak we will know how to find and remove any hindrance if there is one—and how to rest in loving peace when there is none, since God then is only inviting us to move forward to greater maturity, relying on His faithfulness alone.

Questions

1. The earnest desire to do, and not just know, the will of God is a necessary condition for guidance. Discuss.

2. What is the difference, if any, between: (a) not planning to be guided by God; and (b) planning not to be guided by God.

3. Does the lack of specific guidance on a matter mean that one is "out of God's will"? Why?

4. Explain the incompatibility of the following two notions:
   (a) life at its best (and thus guidance) seen as a conversational relationship between two persons (God and you); and
   (b) the "perfect will of God" is specific for all occasions and its absence implies some defect in the believer.

5. Is it right to expect that adequate guidance will put a person "beyond risk" in their decisions in life? Why?

6. "An obsession with 'guidance' is idolatry." Discuss.

7. How should one go about seeking "guidance about guidance"?

8. What is there "beyond guidance" for the Christian to seek?

Notes

1. John Wood Oman, *Grace and Personality* (Cambridge: University Press, 1931).

2. G. Campbell Morgan, *How to Live* (Chicago: Moody Press, n.d.), p. 76.

3. In a radio broadcast December 3, 1982, on "The Will of God." See also the excellent chapter "Interpretations of Impressions," in Dobson's *Emotions: Can You Trust Them?* (Ventura, CA: Regal Books, 1981).

4. F.B. Meyer, *The Secret of Guidance* (Chicago: Moody Press, n.d.), p. 43.

5. John Wood Oman, Op. Cit.

6. W.R. Sorley, *The Moral Life* (Cambridge: The University Press, 1911), p. 138.

7. Garry Friesen, *Decision Making and the Will of God* (Portland, OR: Multnomah Press, 1980), p. 145.

8. Brother Lawrence, *The Practice of the Presence of God* (Old Tappan, NJ: Fleming H. Revell Co., 1958), p. 51.

9. A.T. Pierson, *George Müller of Bristol* (New York: The Baker and Taylor Co., 1899), p. 196.

10. Herbert Welch, ed., *Selections from the Writings of Reverend John Wesley* (New York: Eaton & Mains, 1901), p. 138.

INDEX

Index, study questions and chapter sub-titles prepared by Raymond R. Neal.